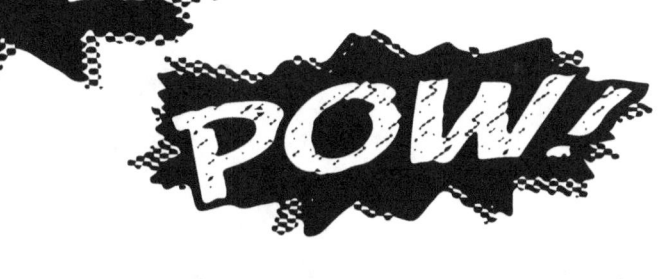

SUPERHEROES

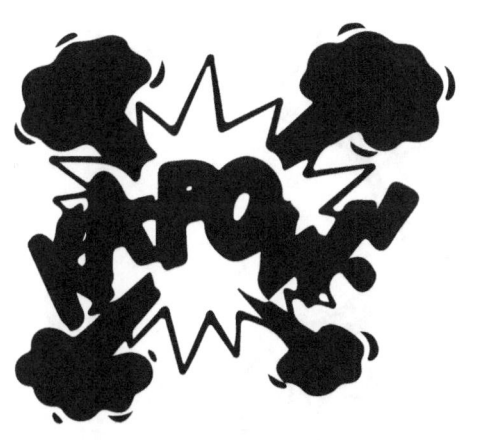

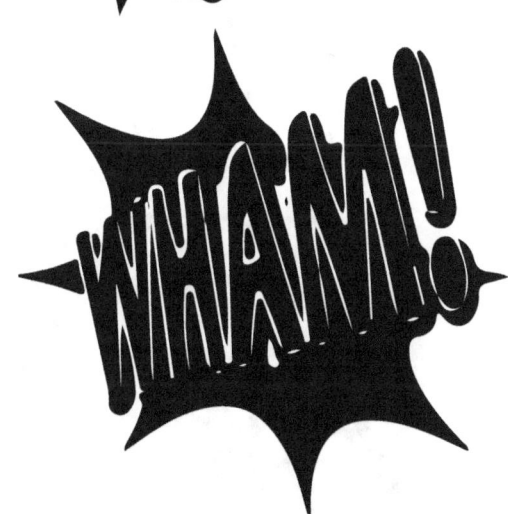

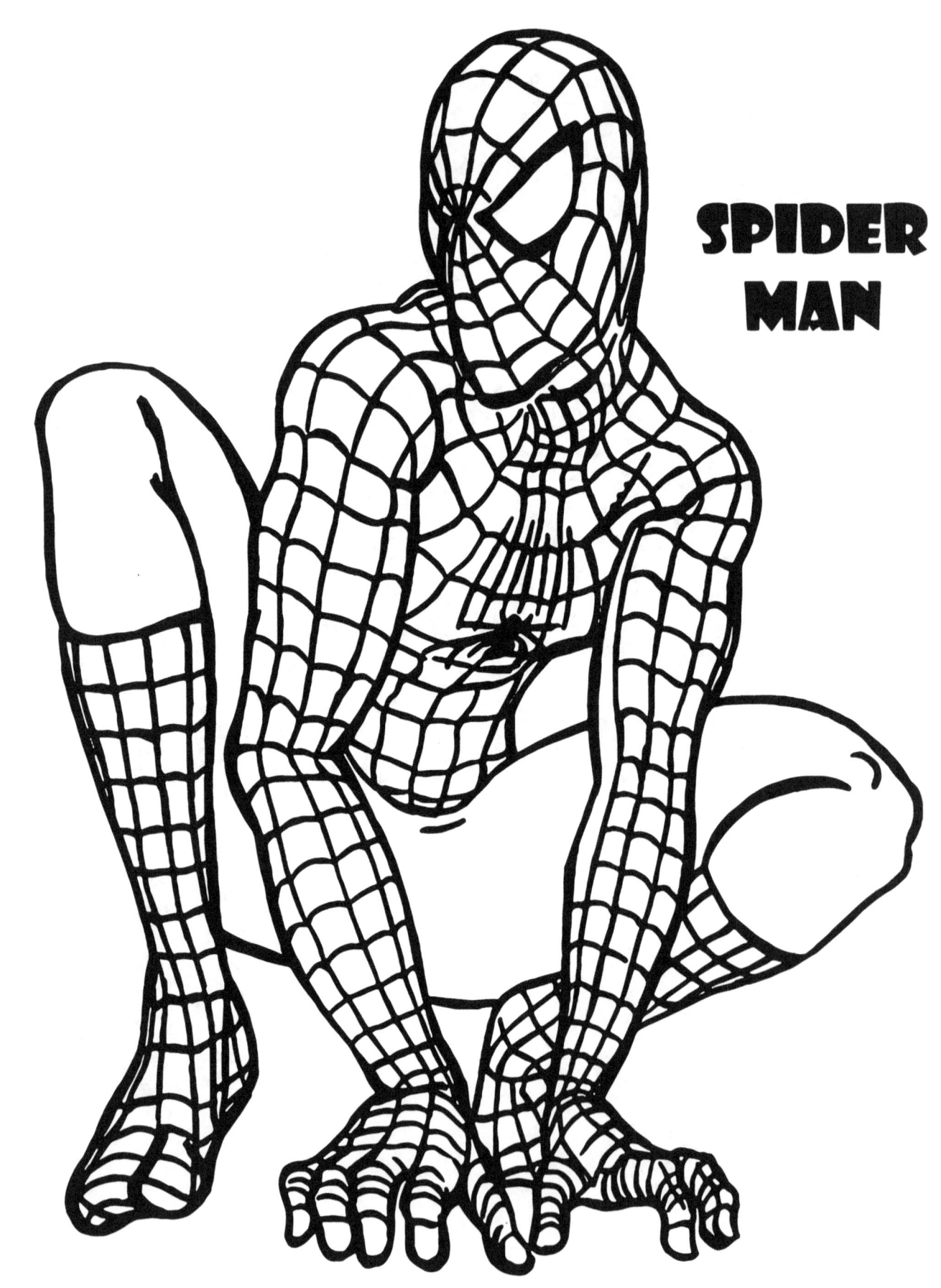

SPIDER
MAN

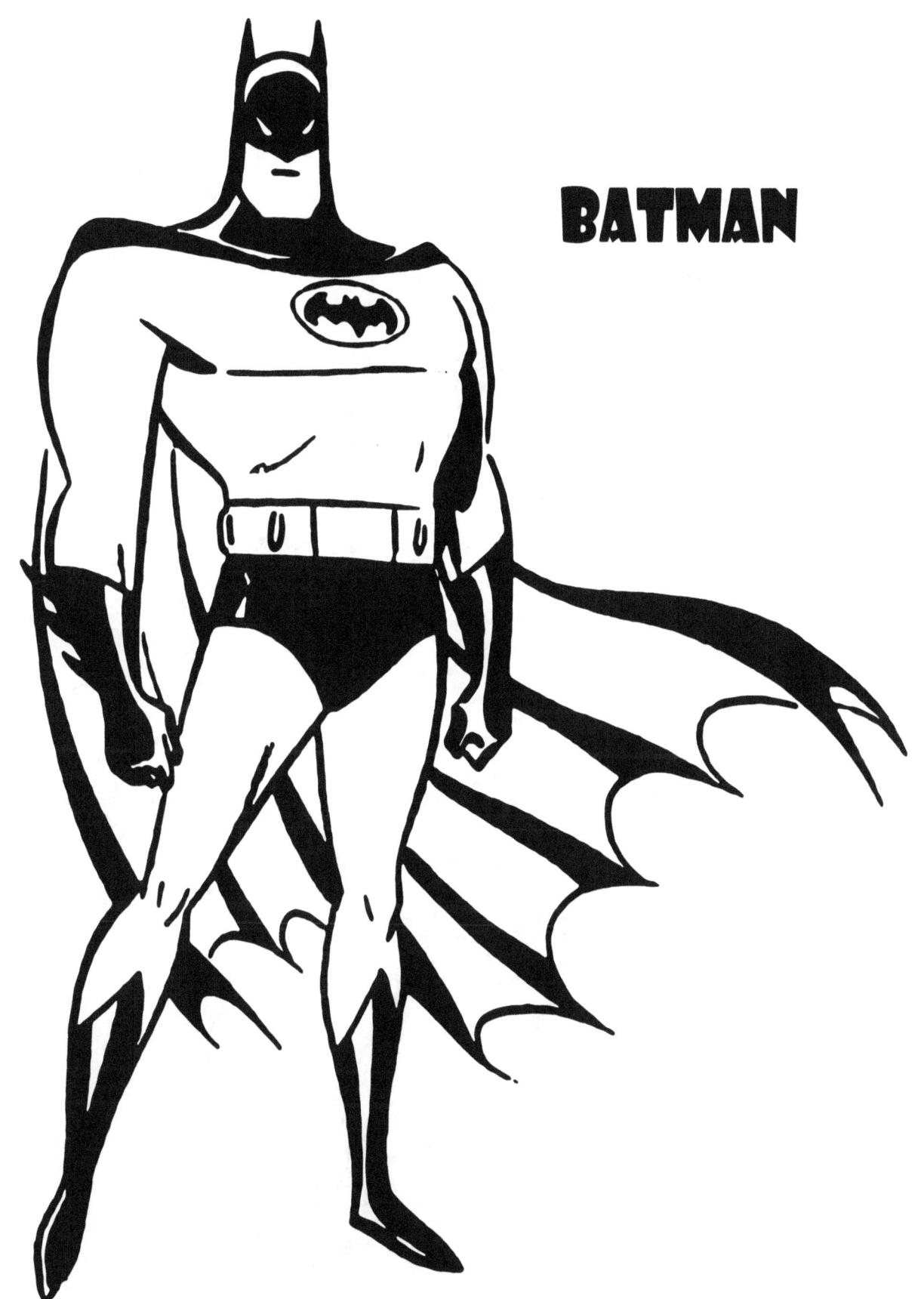

BATMAN

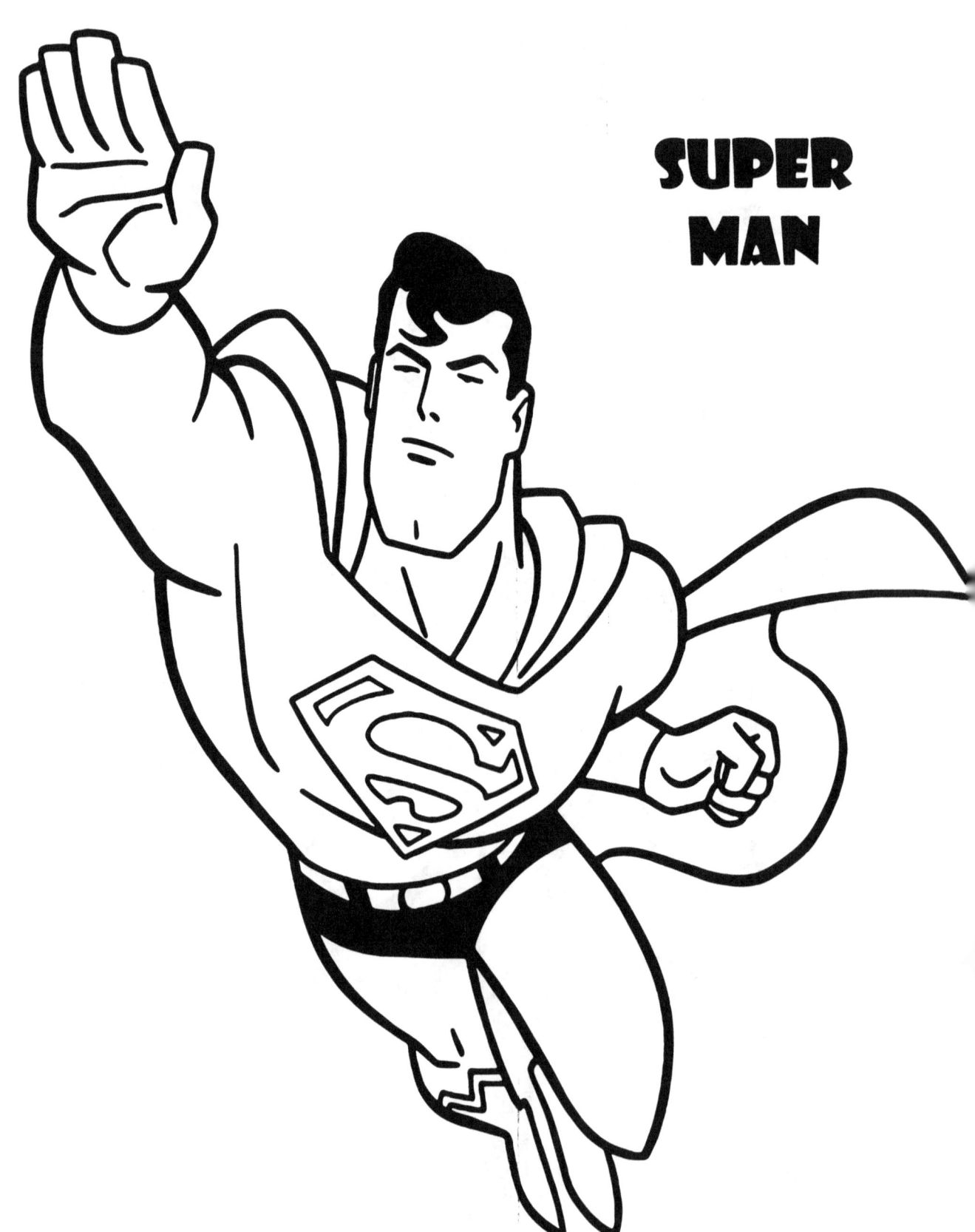

SUPER
MAN

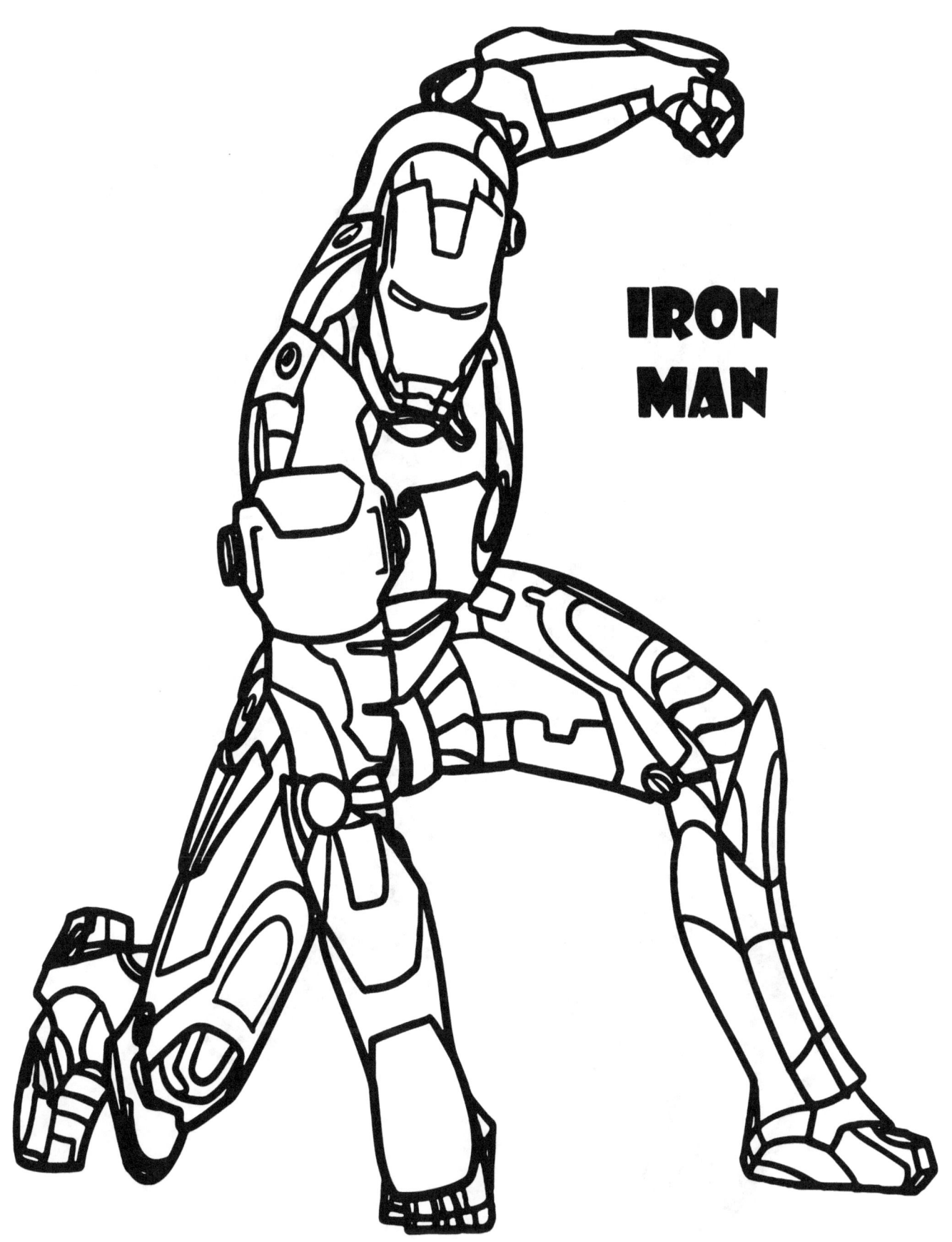

IRON
MAN

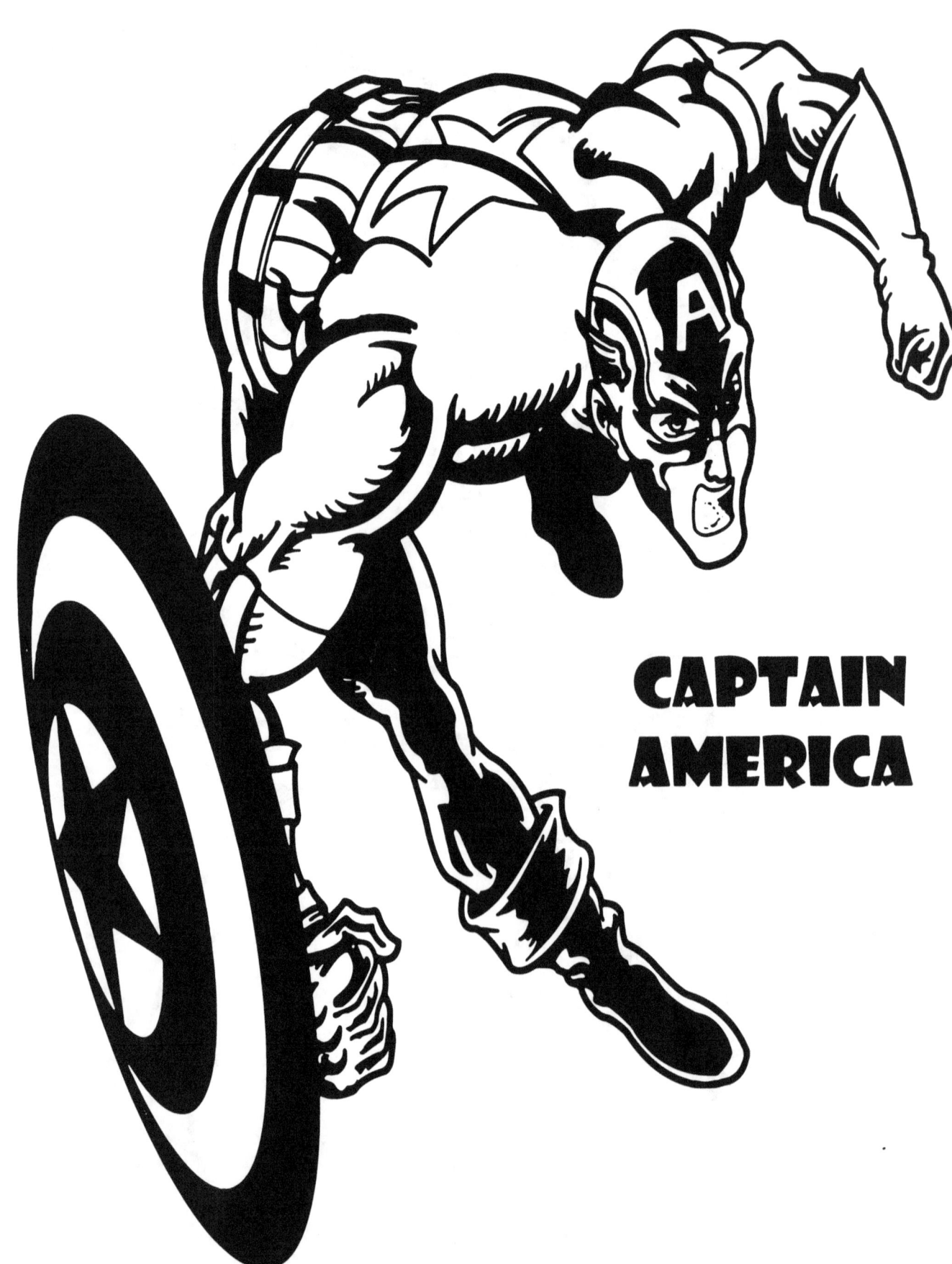

CAPTAIN
AMERICA

HULK

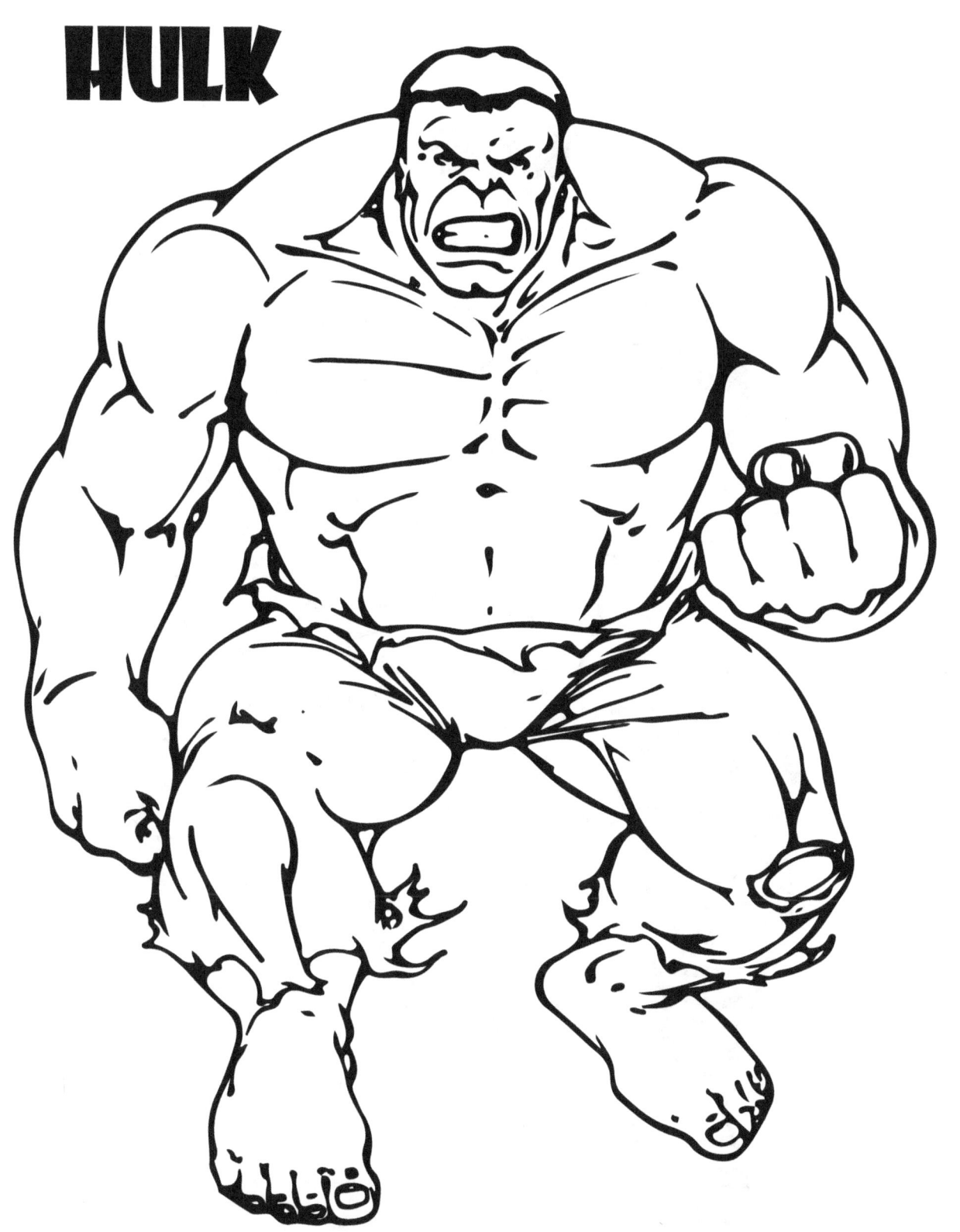

THOR

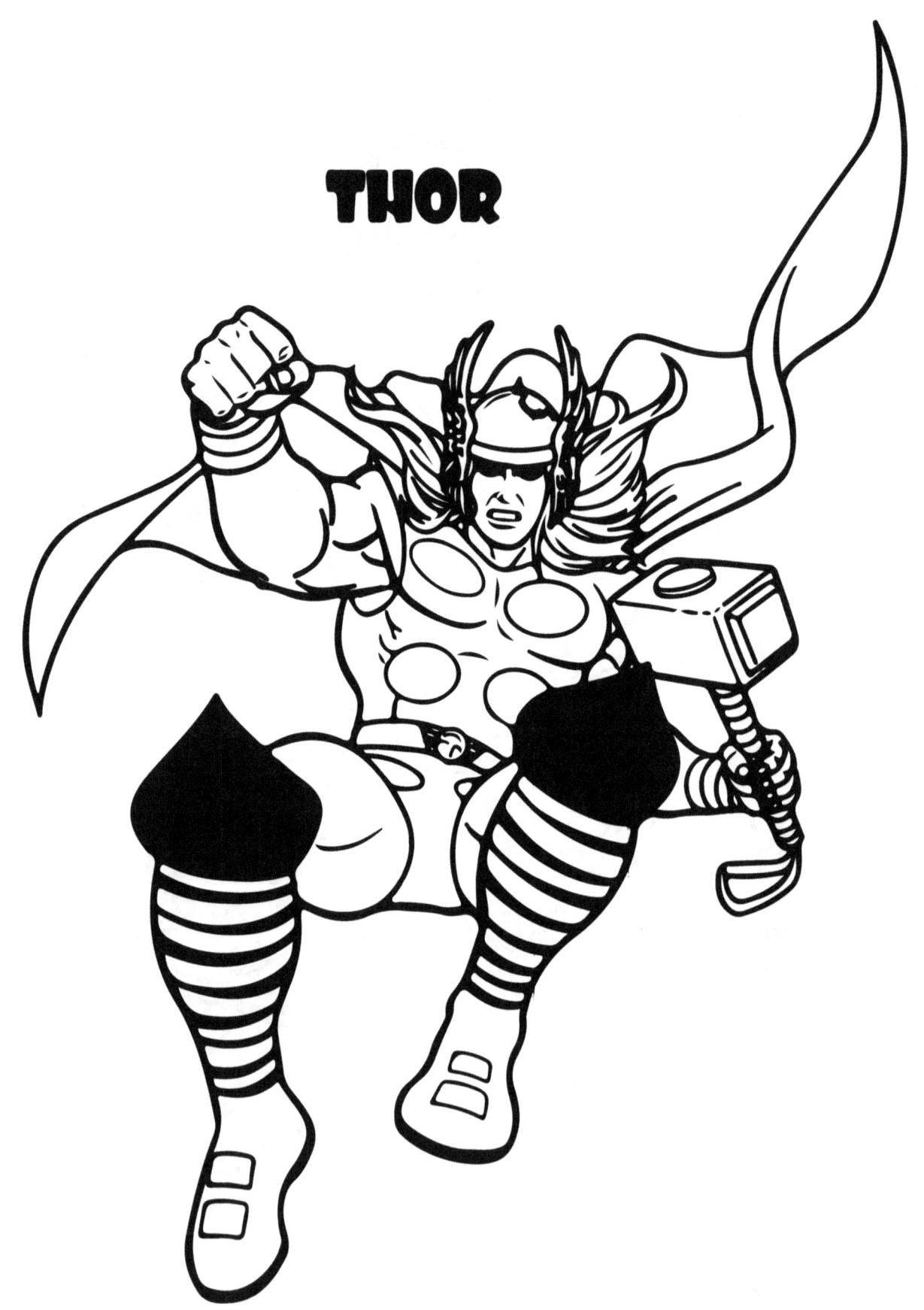

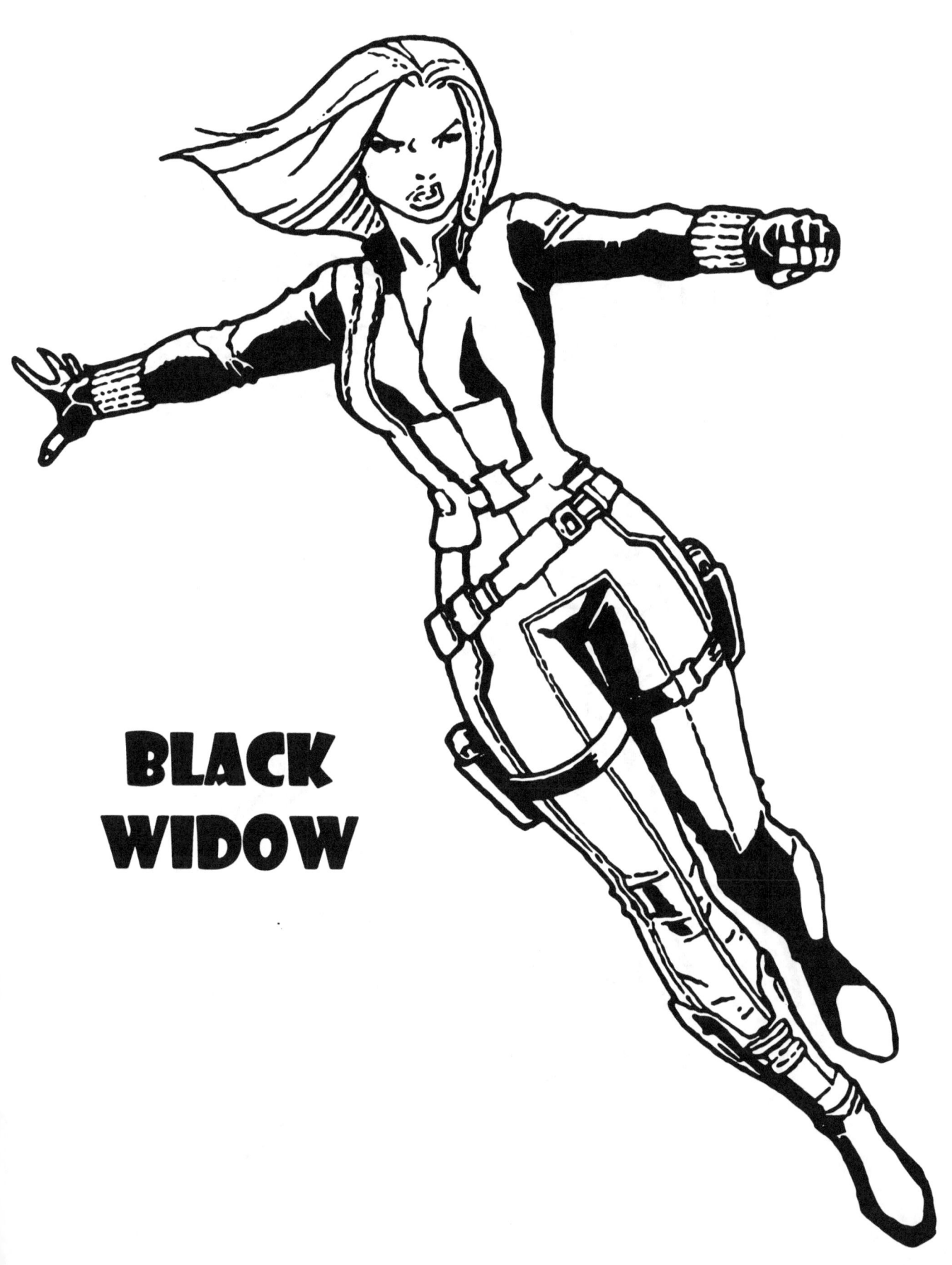

BLACK
WIDOW

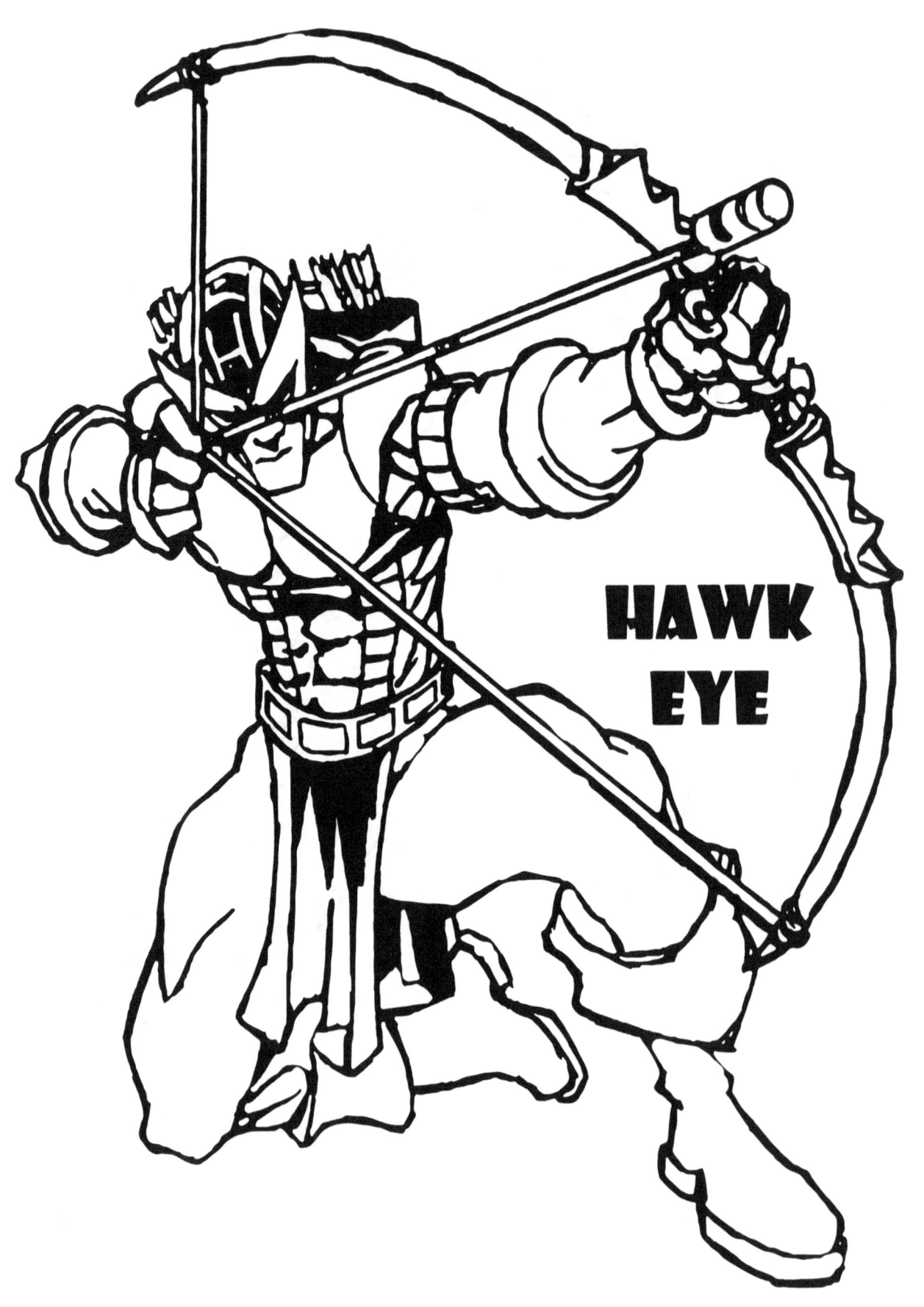

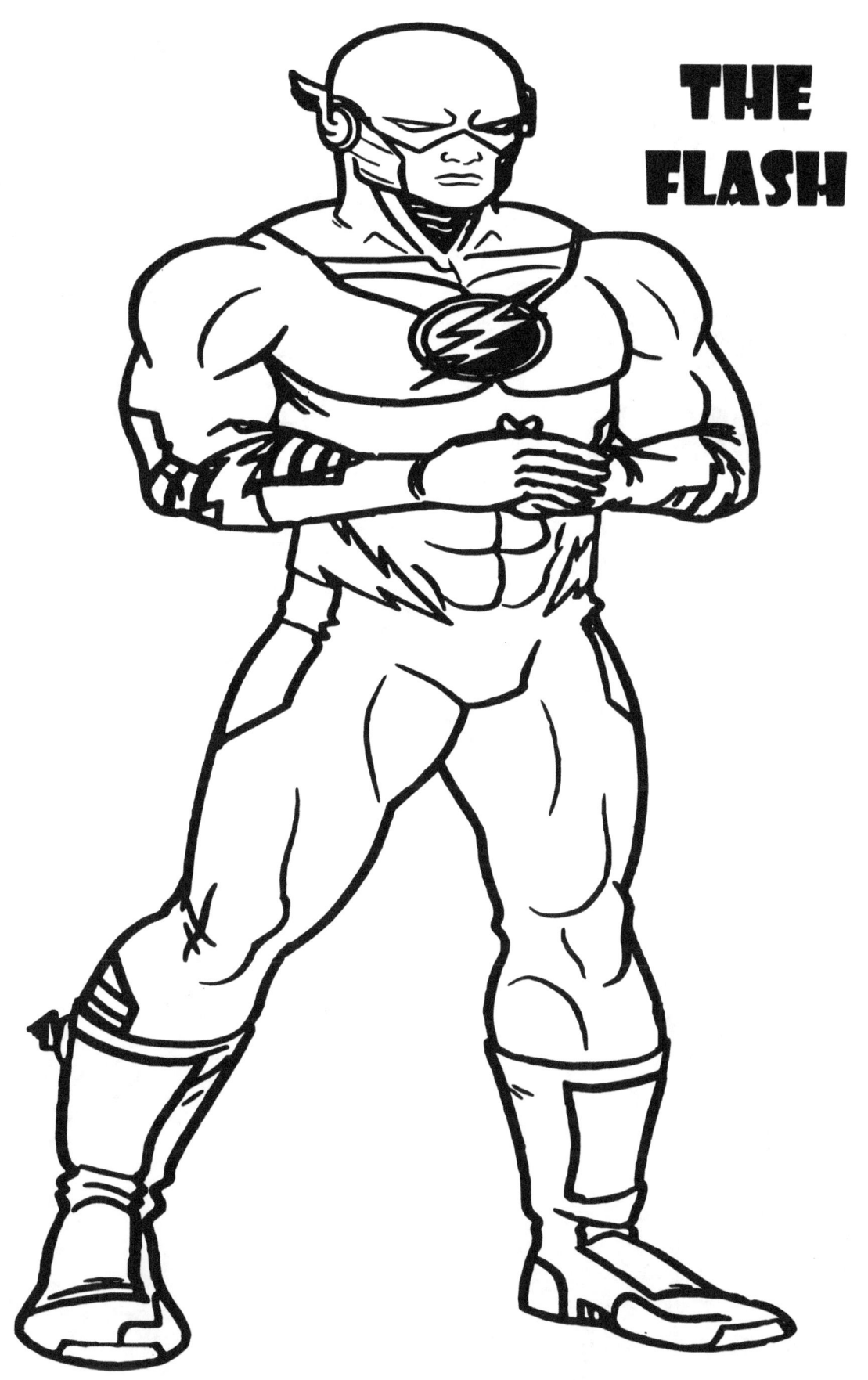

THE
FLASH

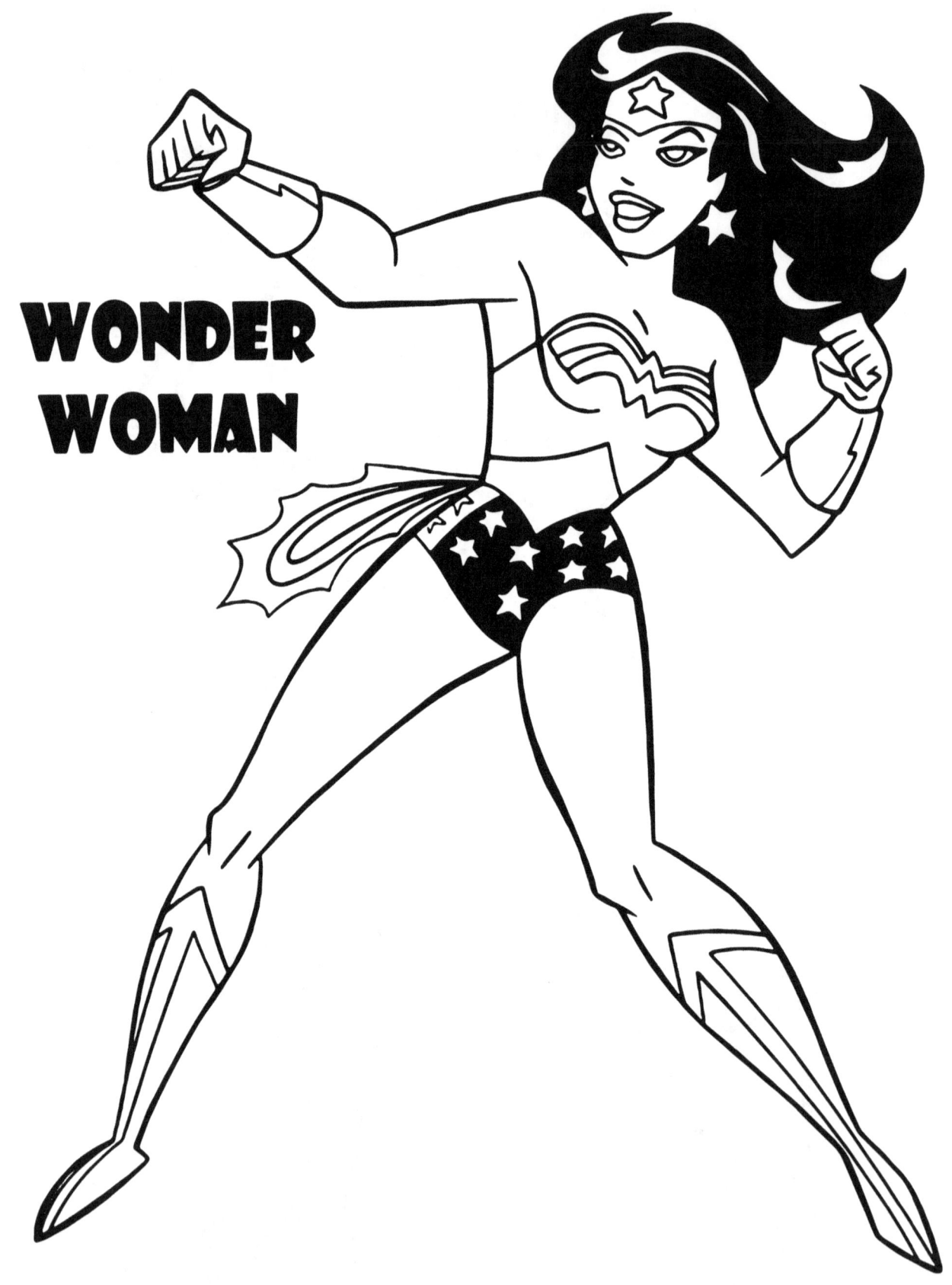

WONDER
WOMAN

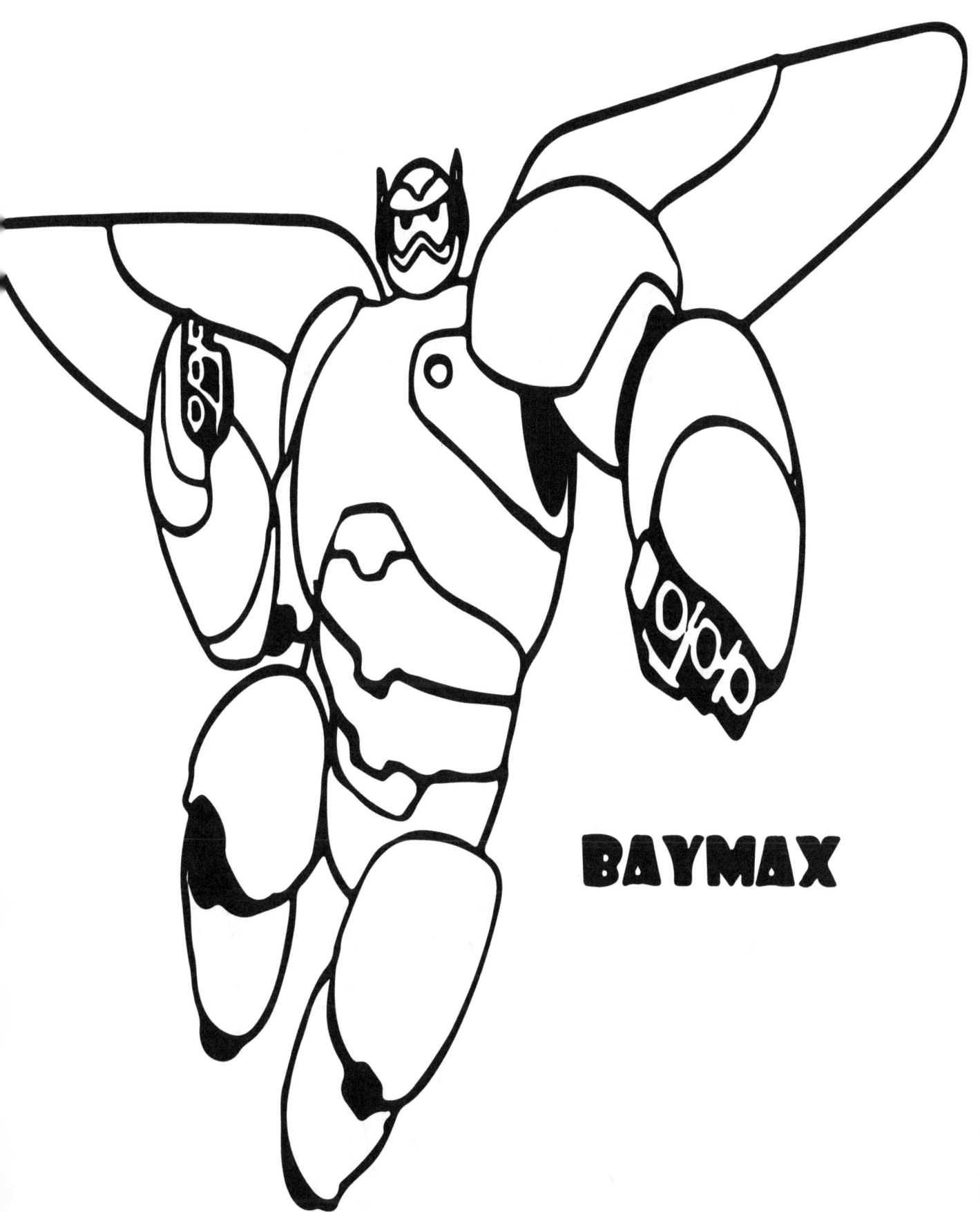

BAYMAX

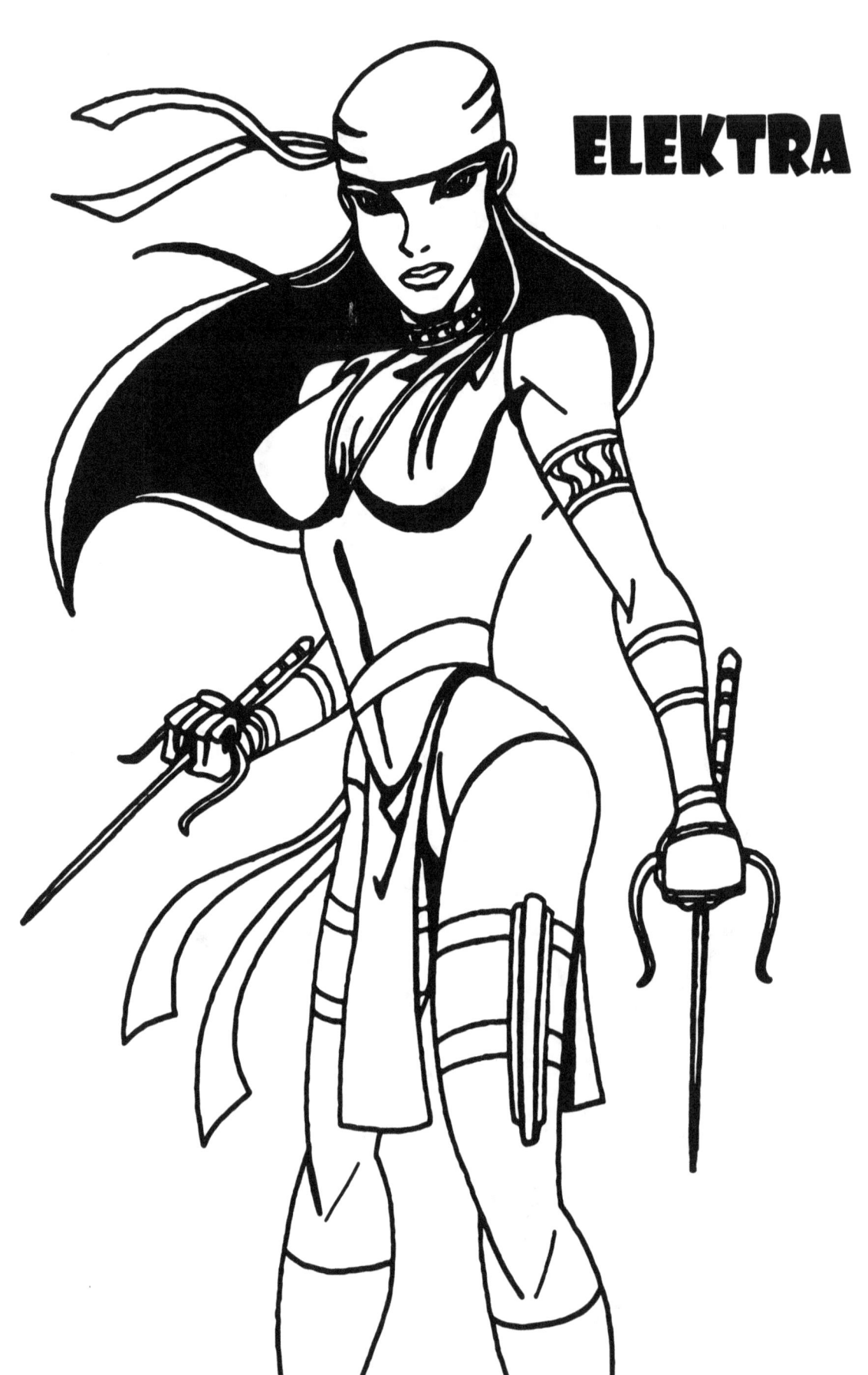

ELEKTRA

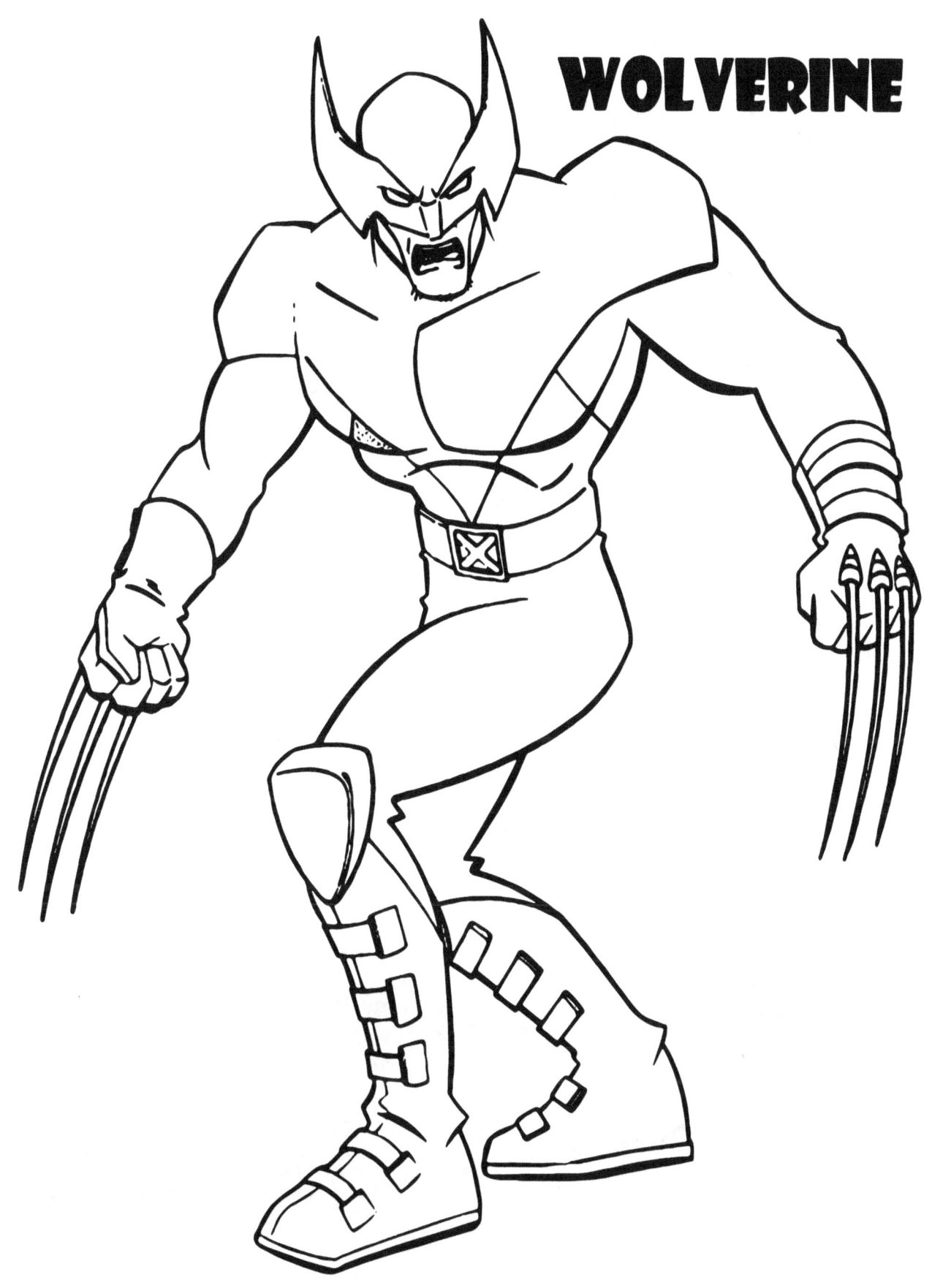

WOLVERINE

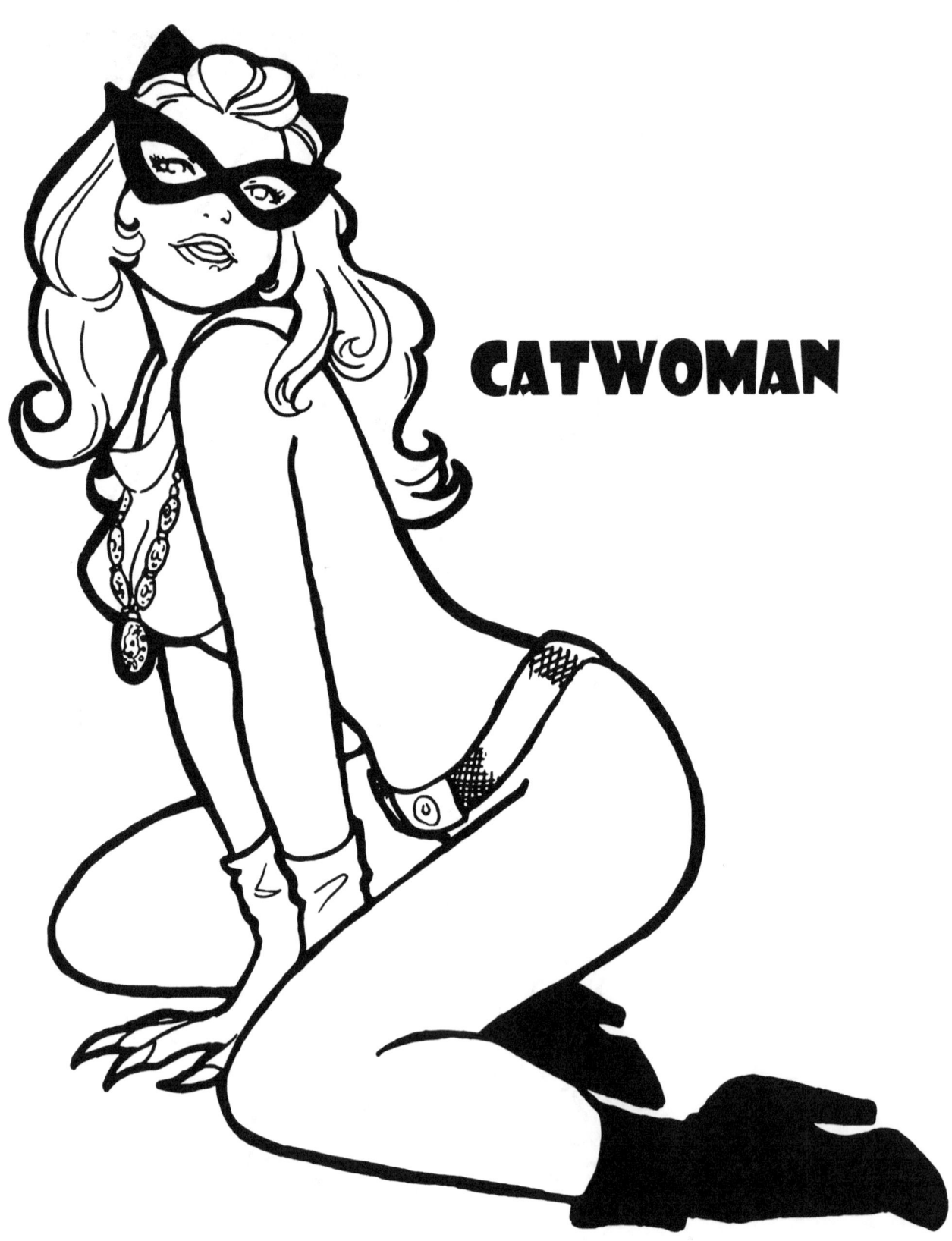

CATWOMAN

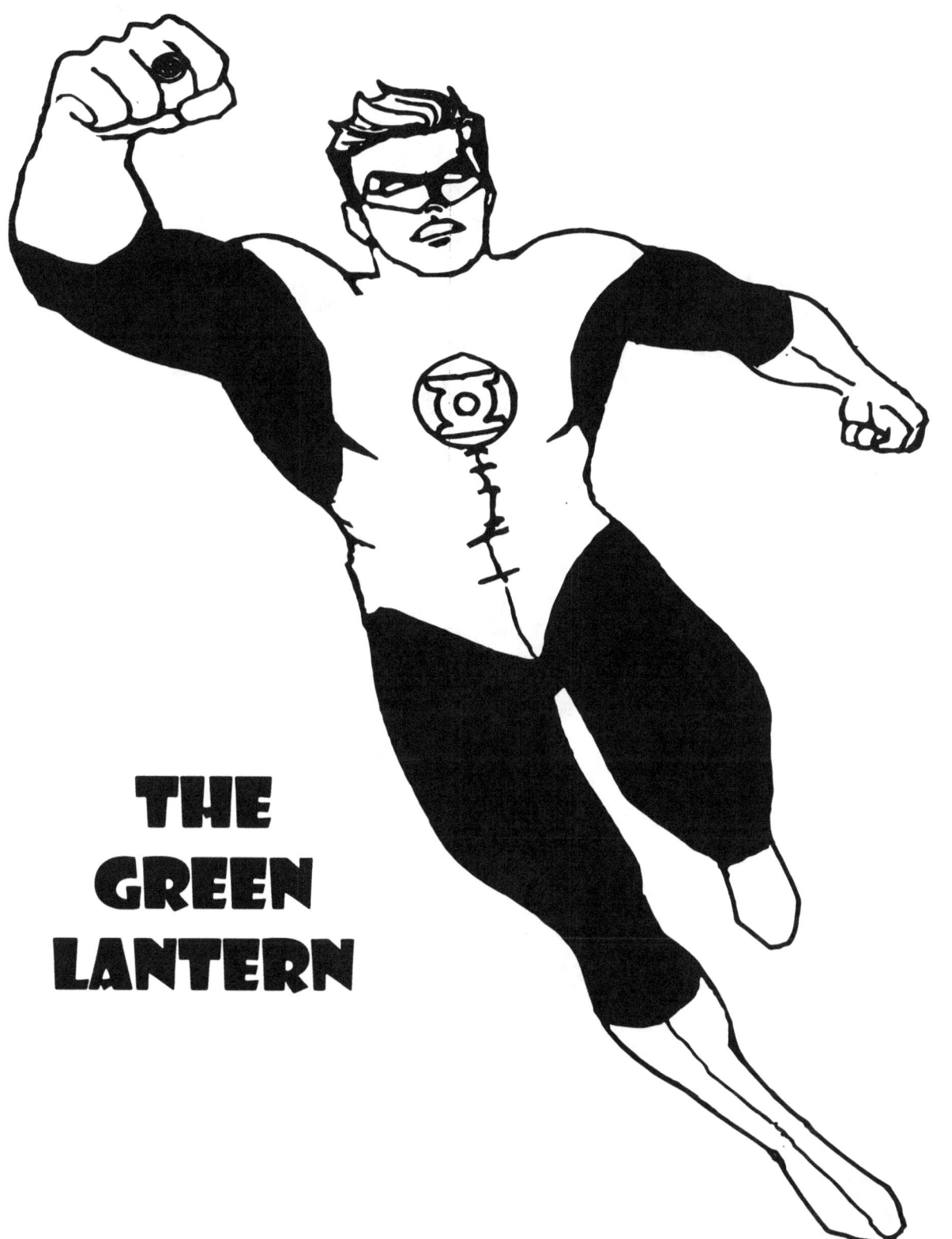

THE
GREEN
LANTERN

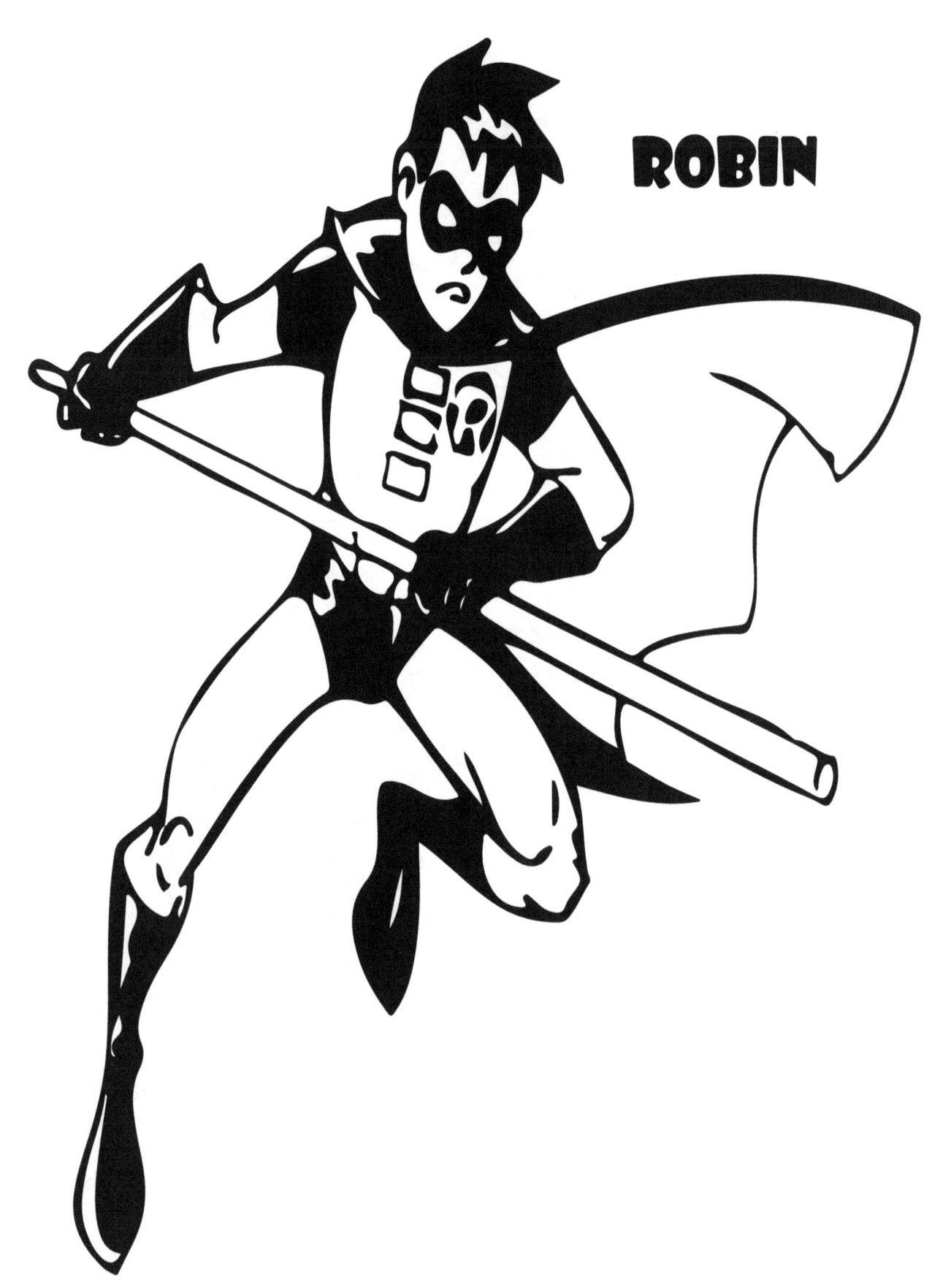

ROBIN

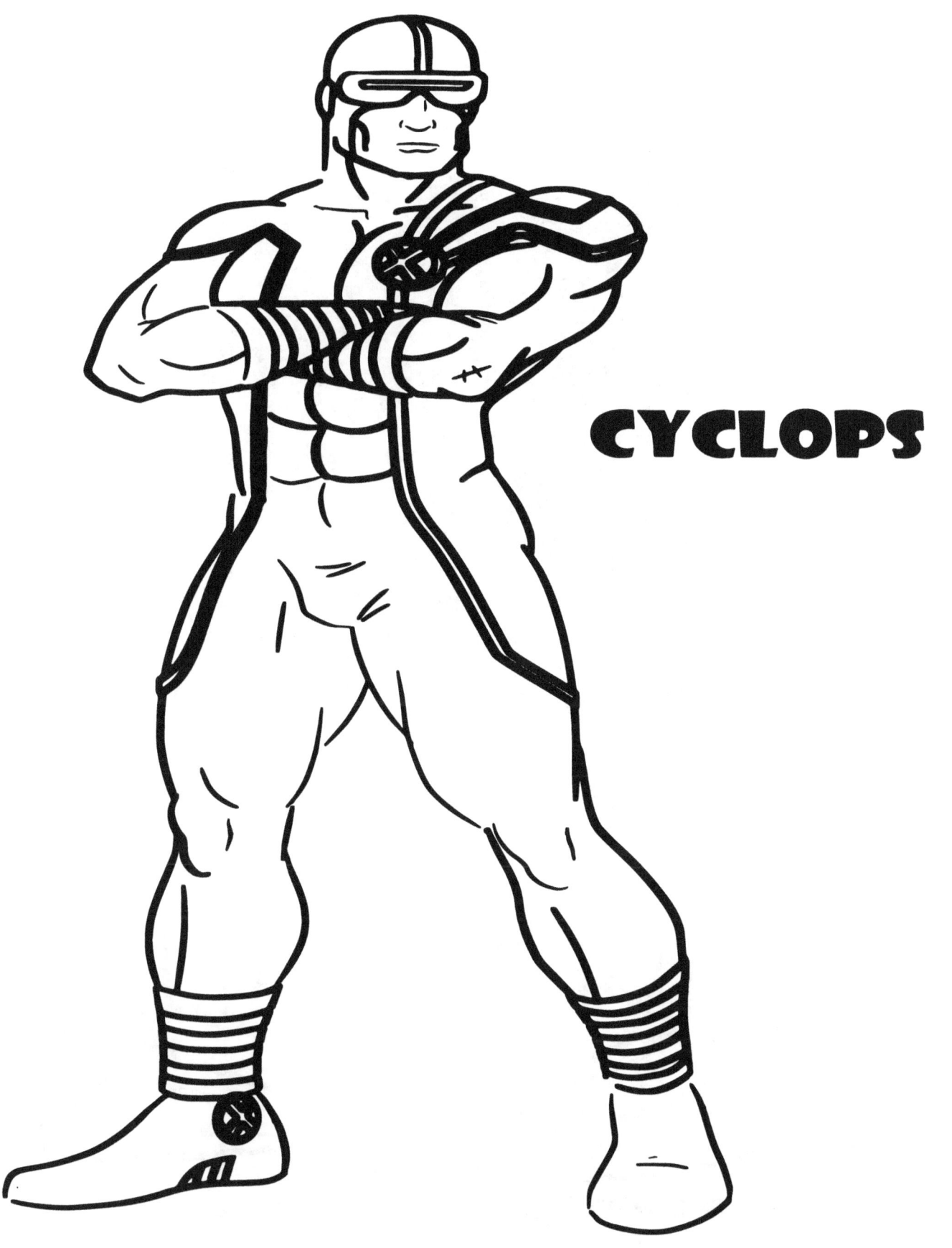

CYCLOPS

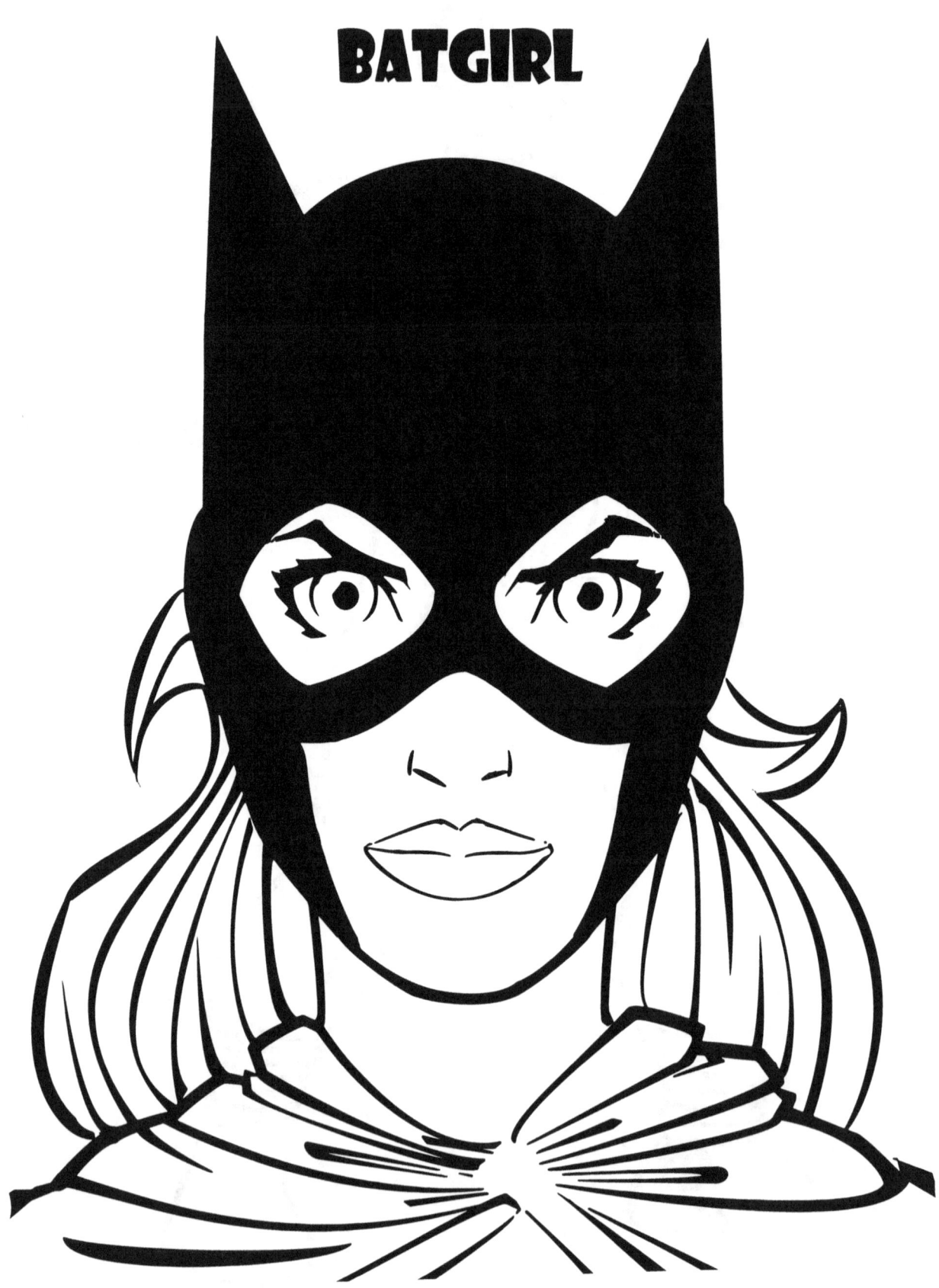

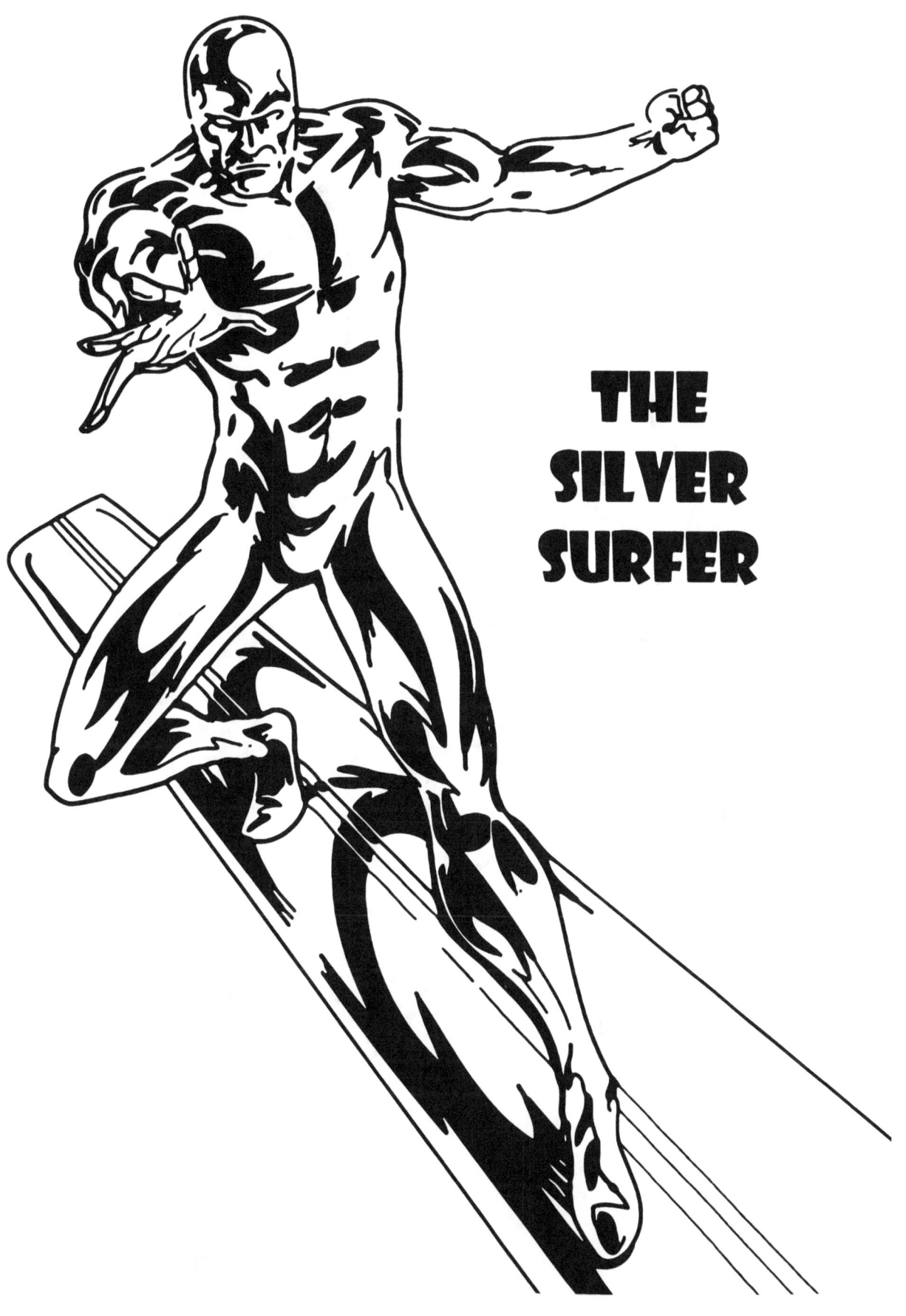

THE SILVER SURFER

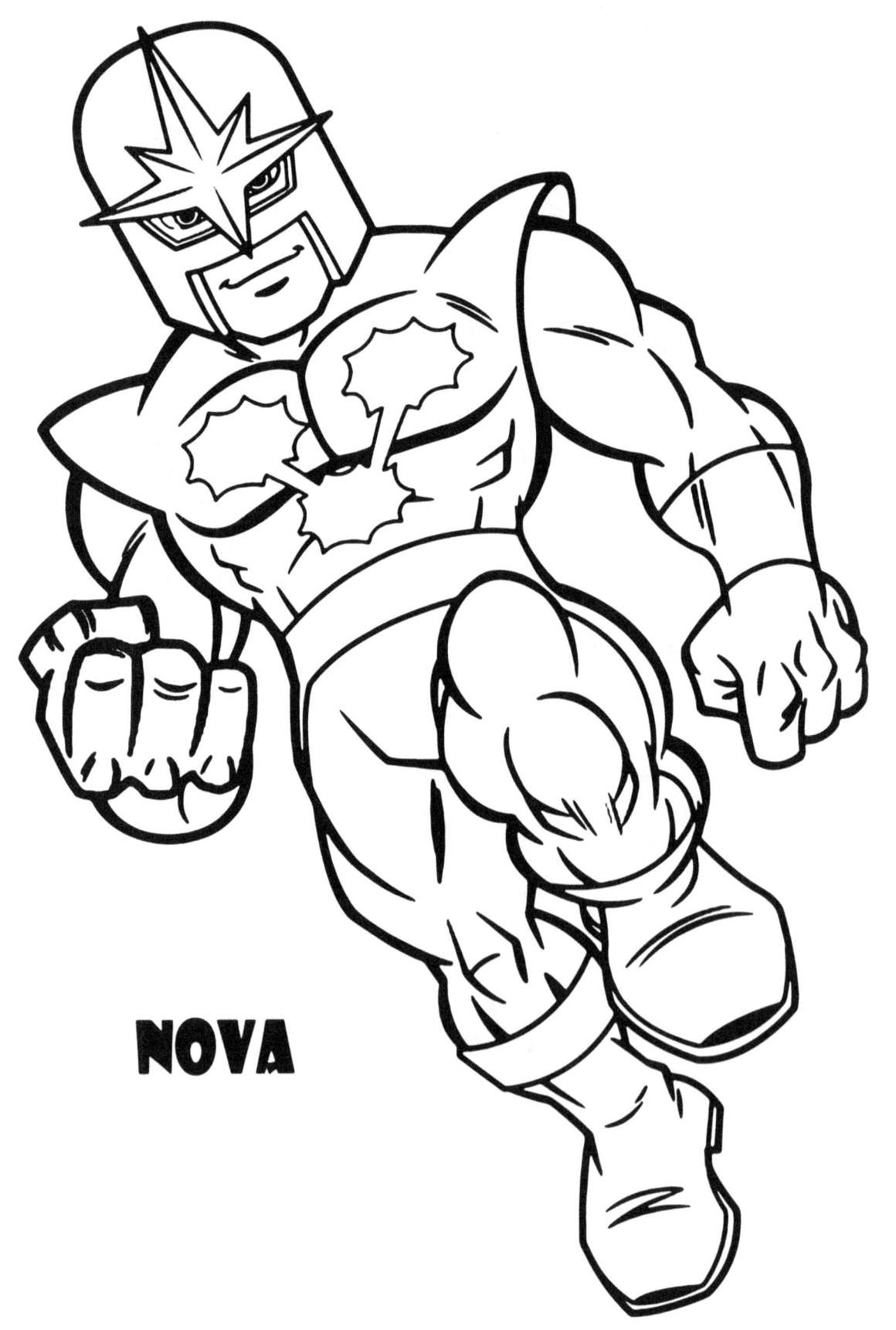

NOVA

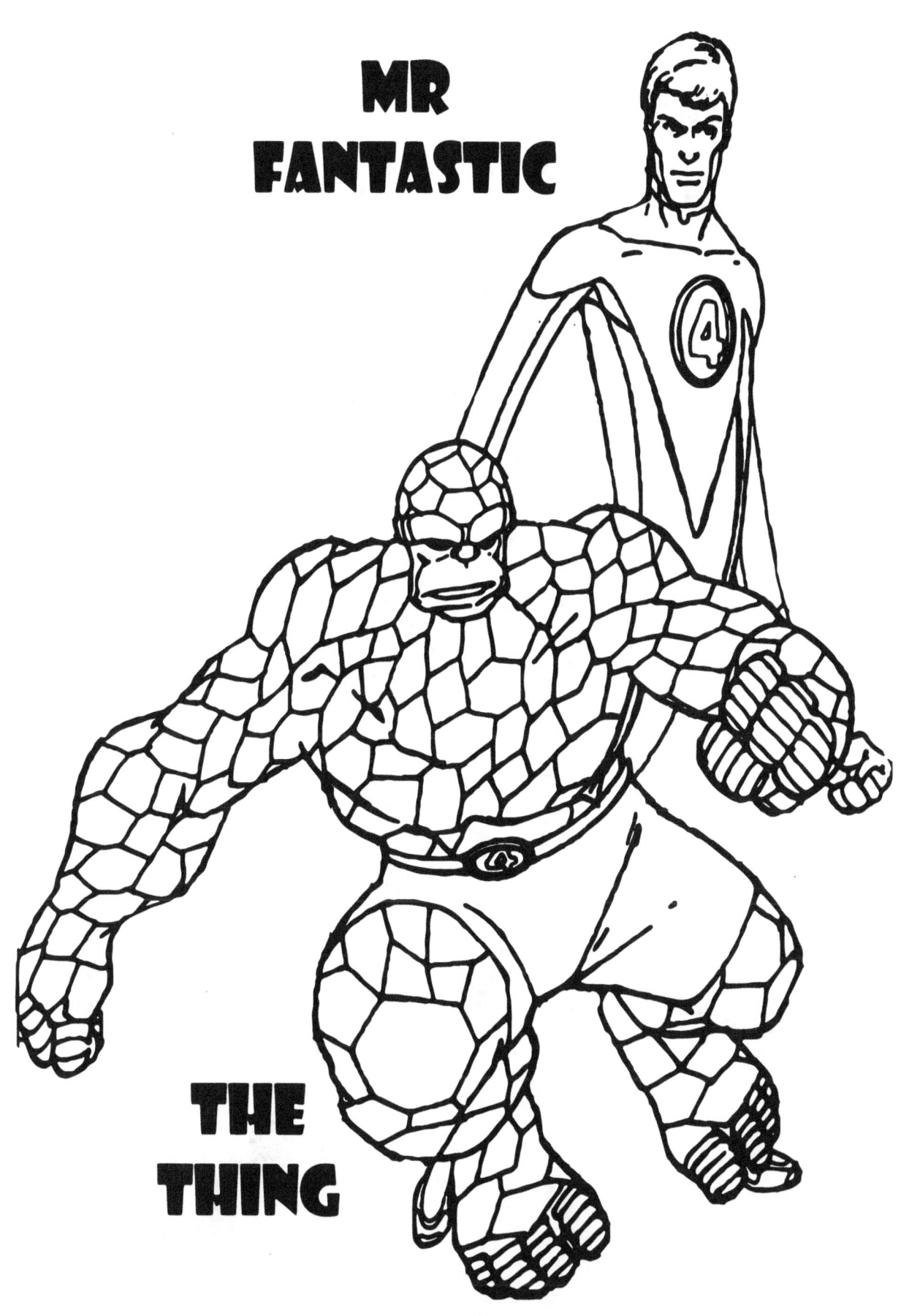

MR INCREDIBLE

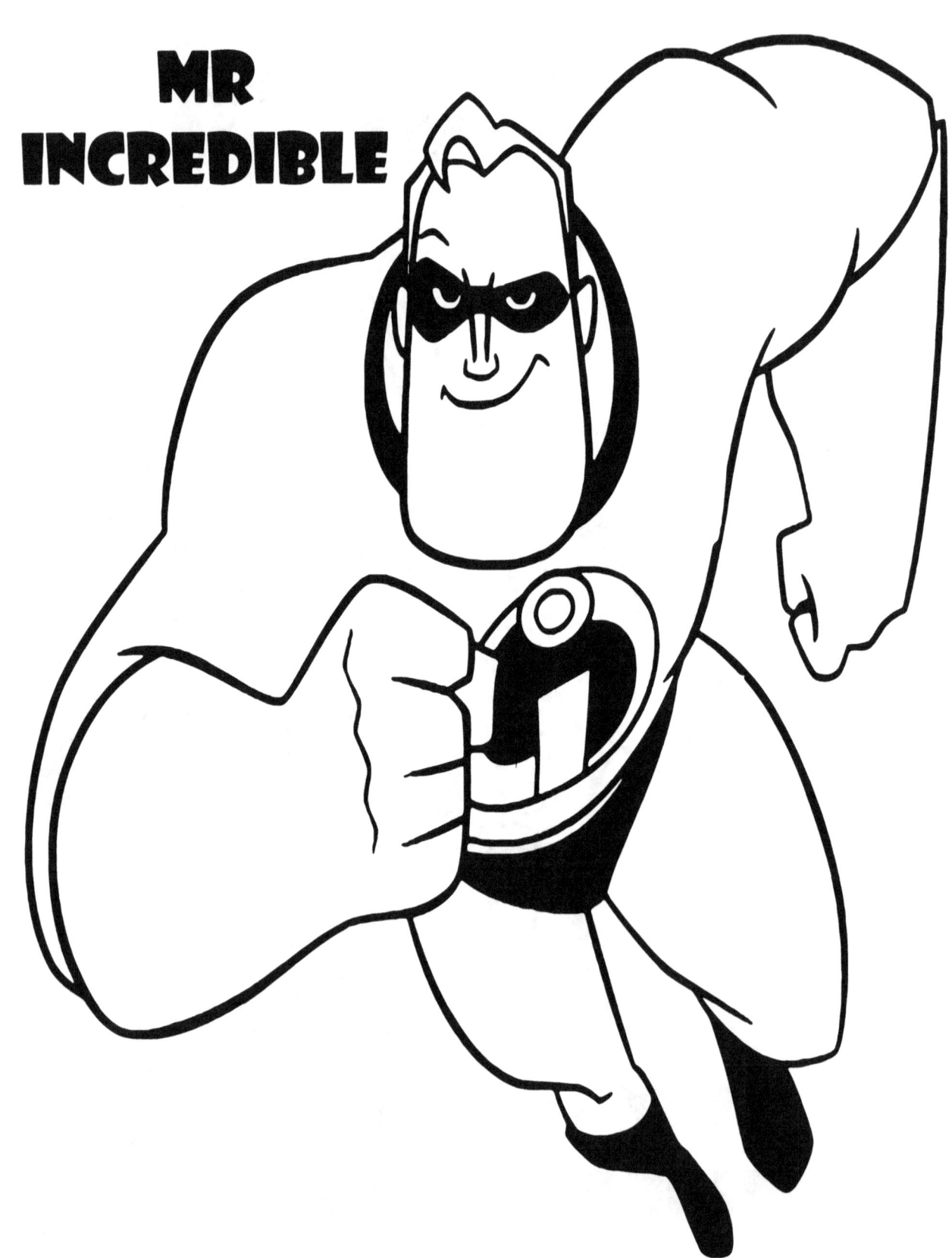

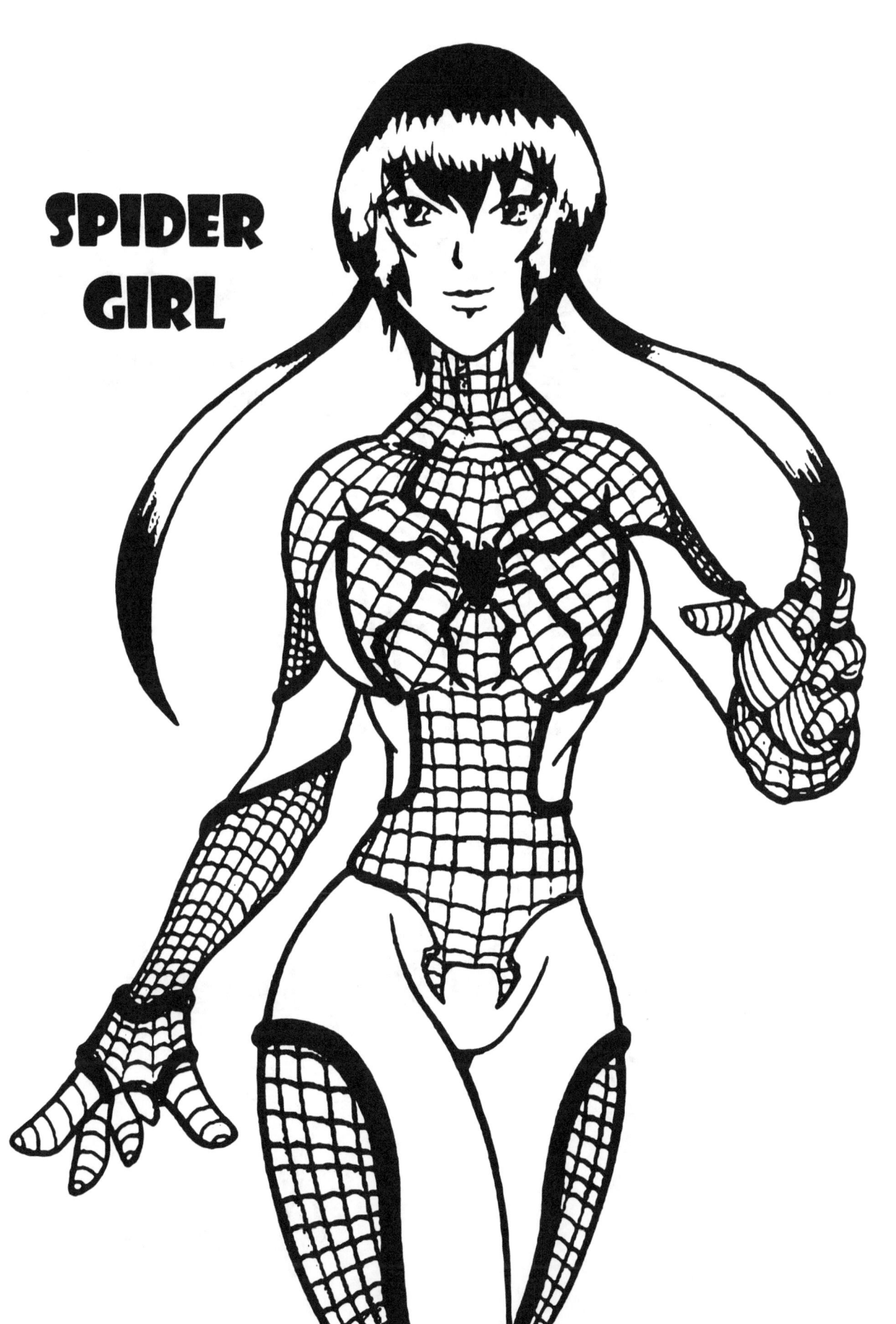

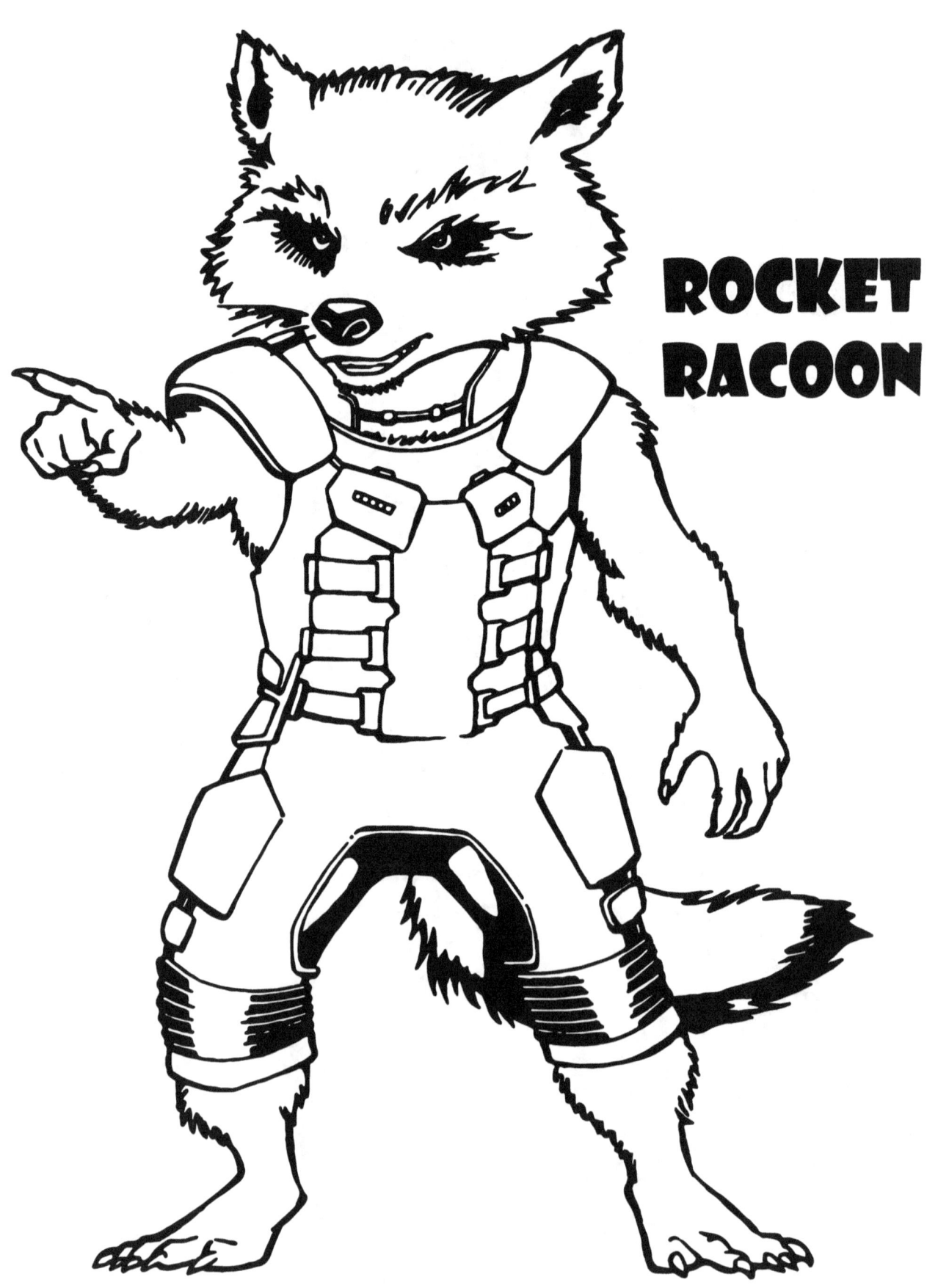

ROCKET
RACOON

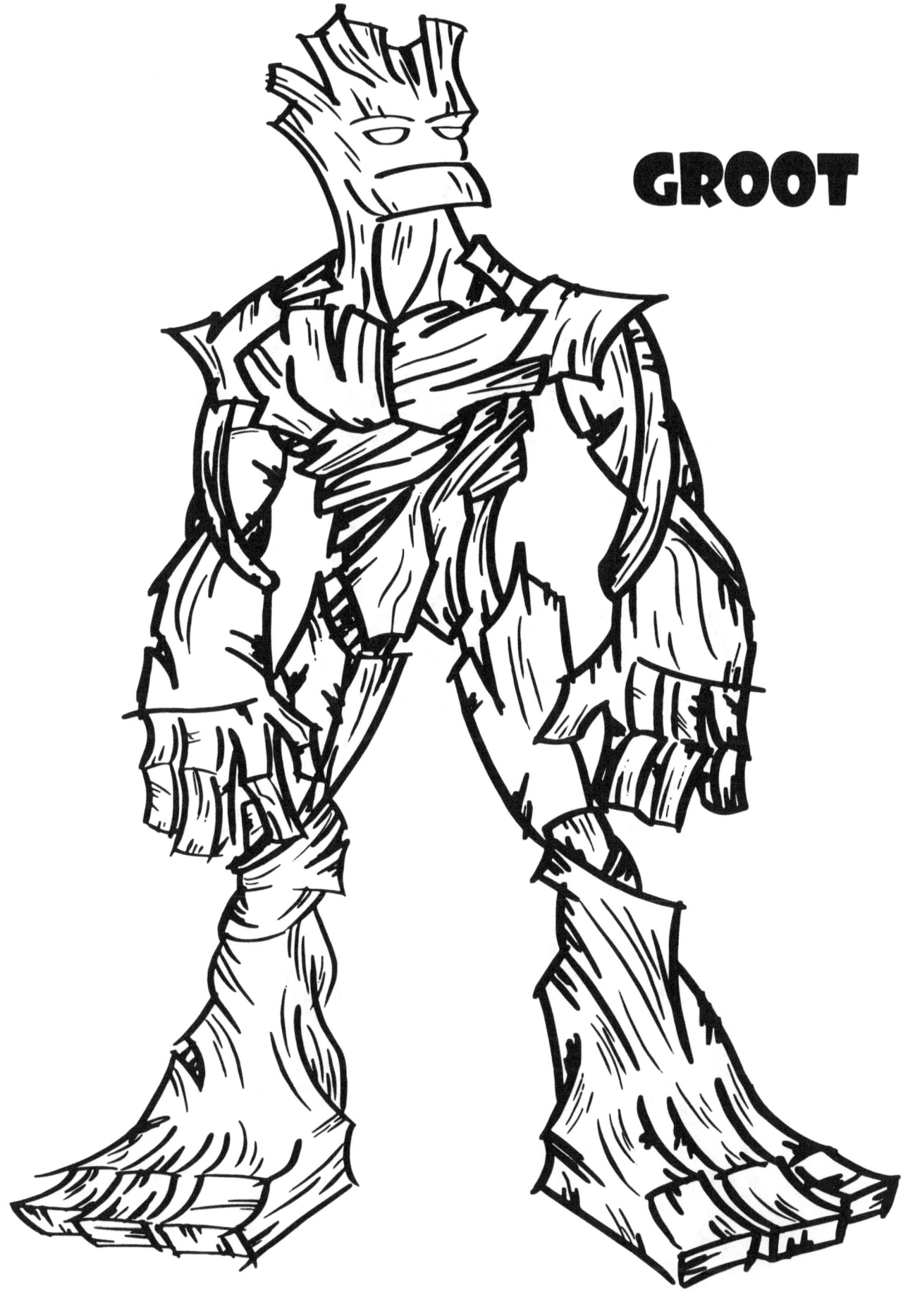

GROOT

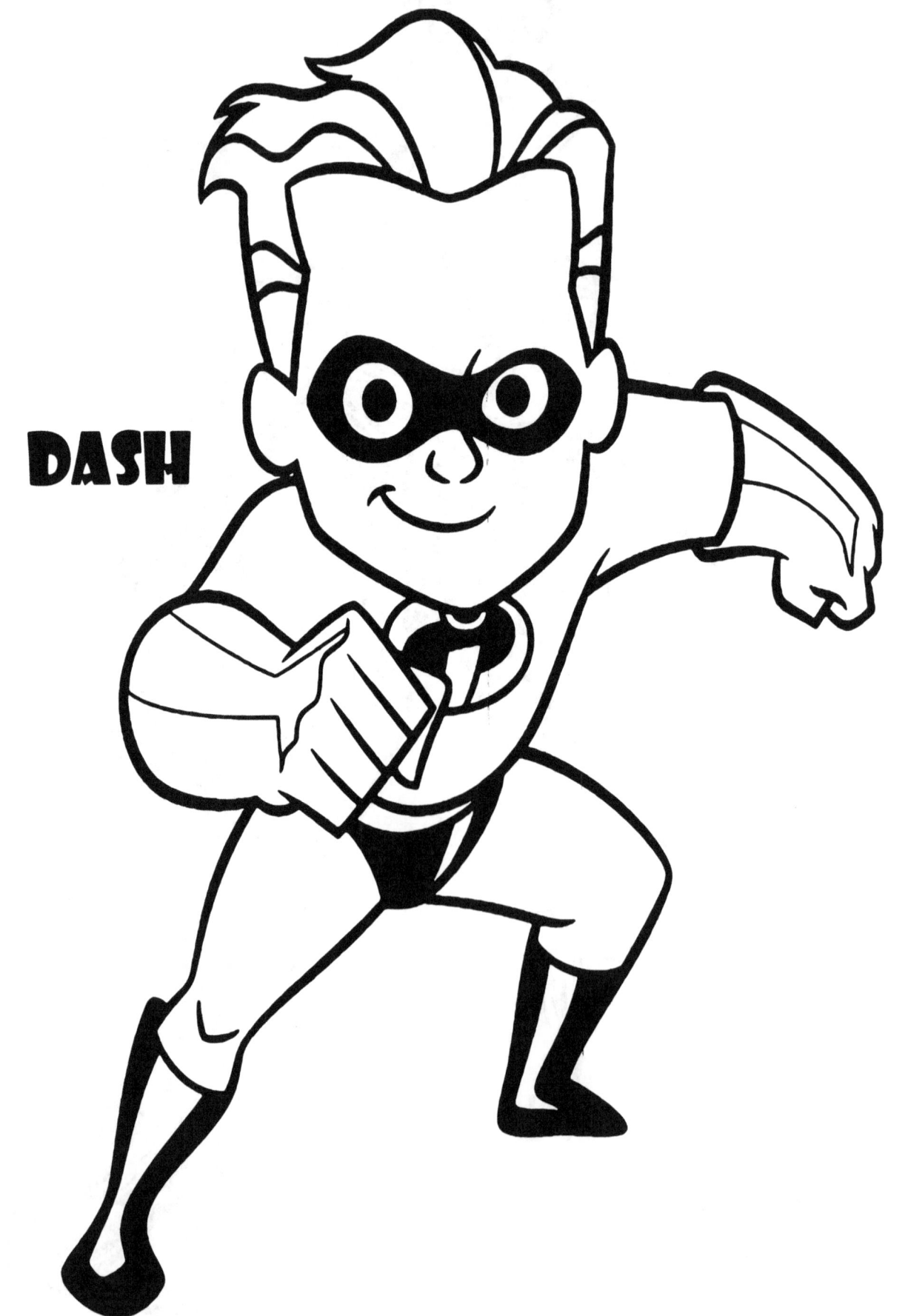

DASH

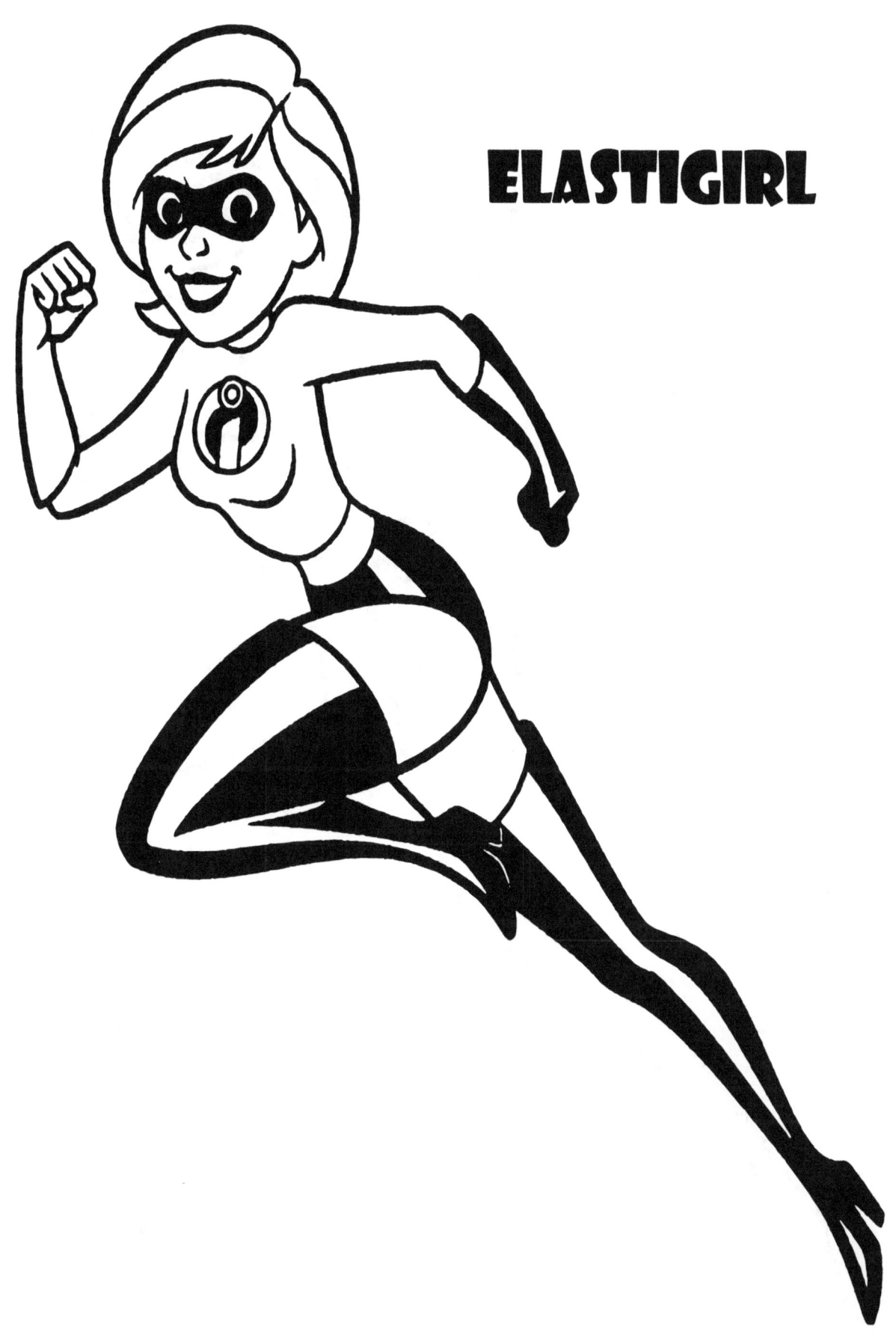

ELASTIGIRL

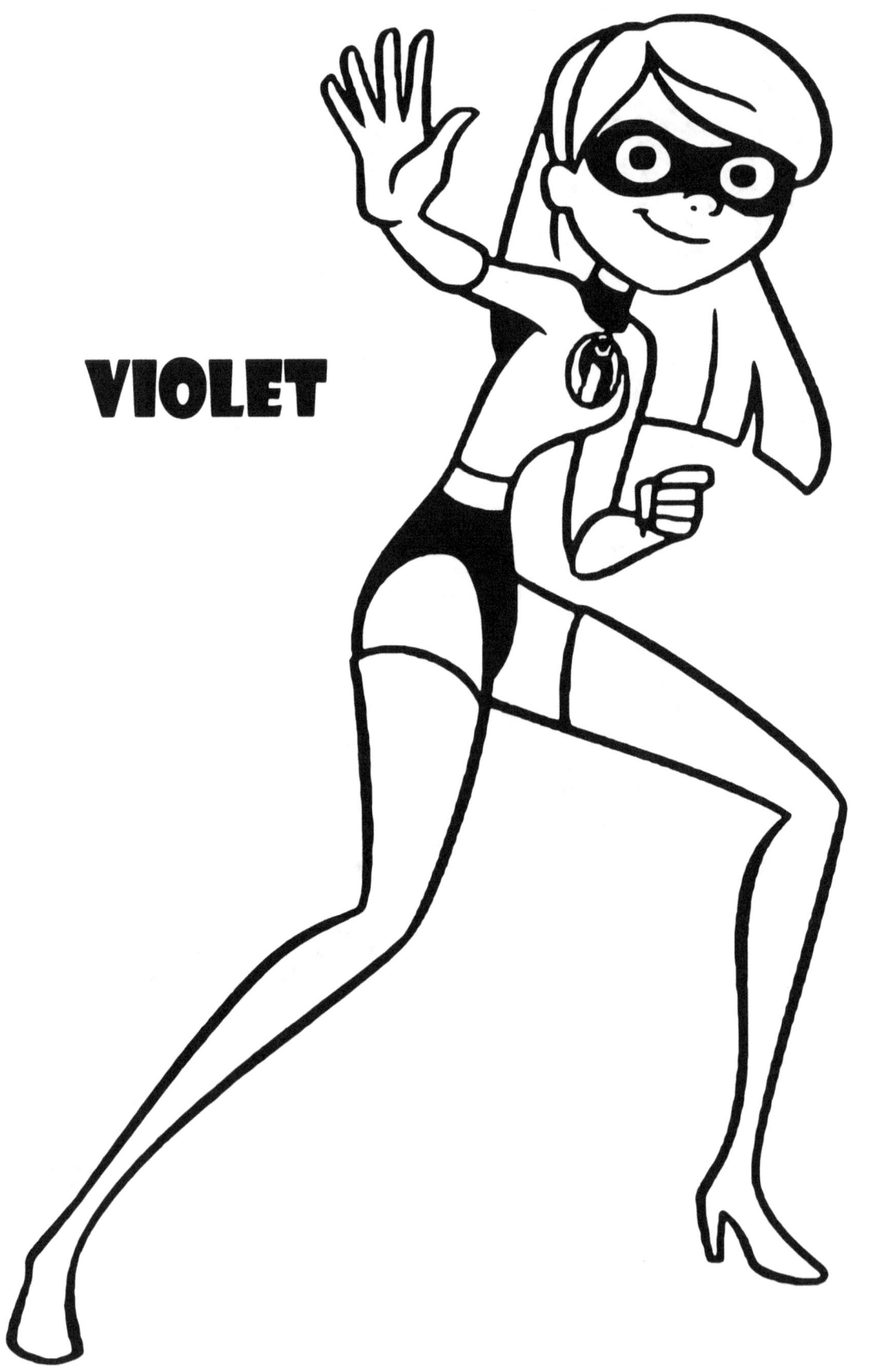

VIOLET

MARTIAN MANHUNTER

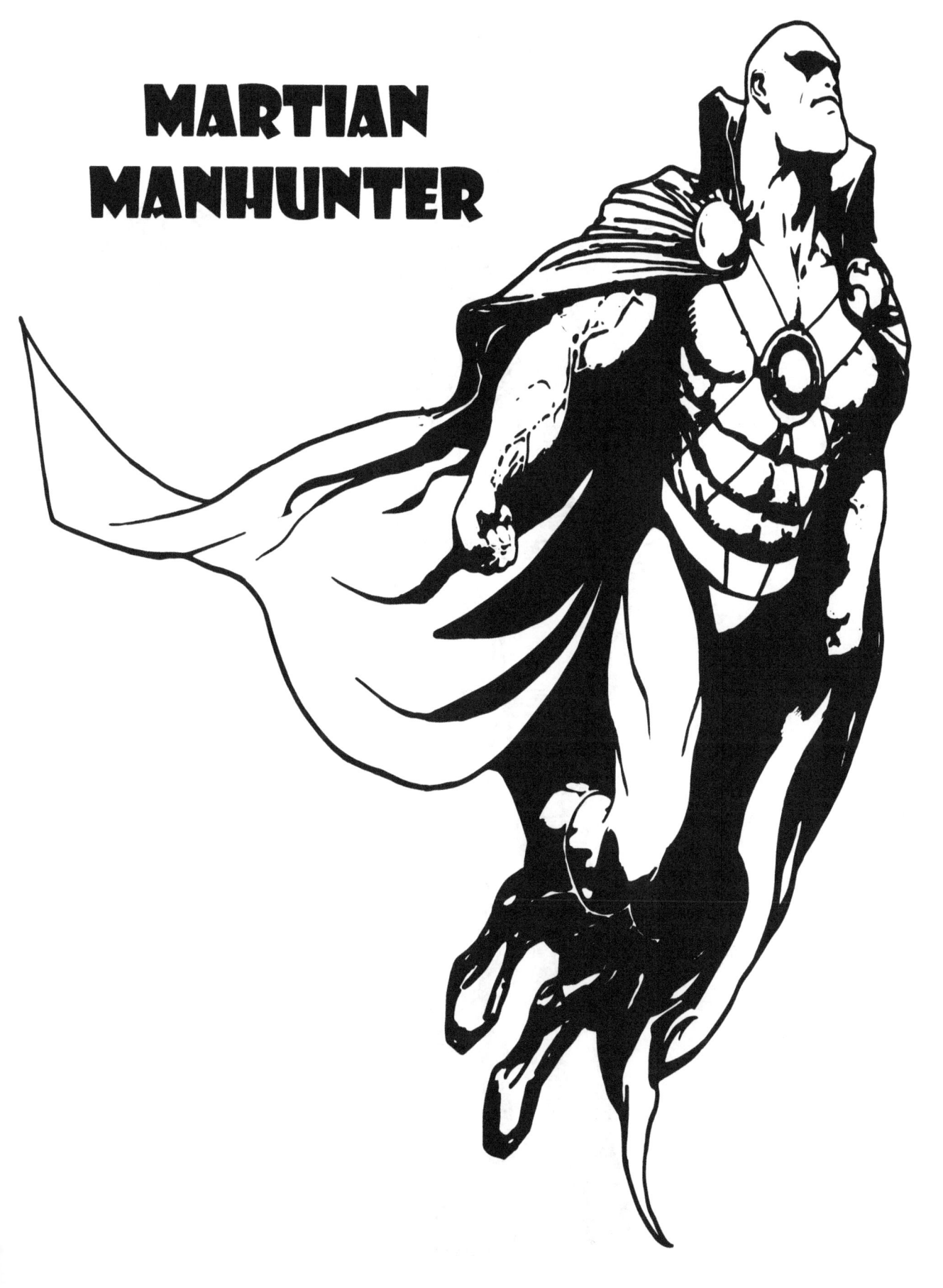

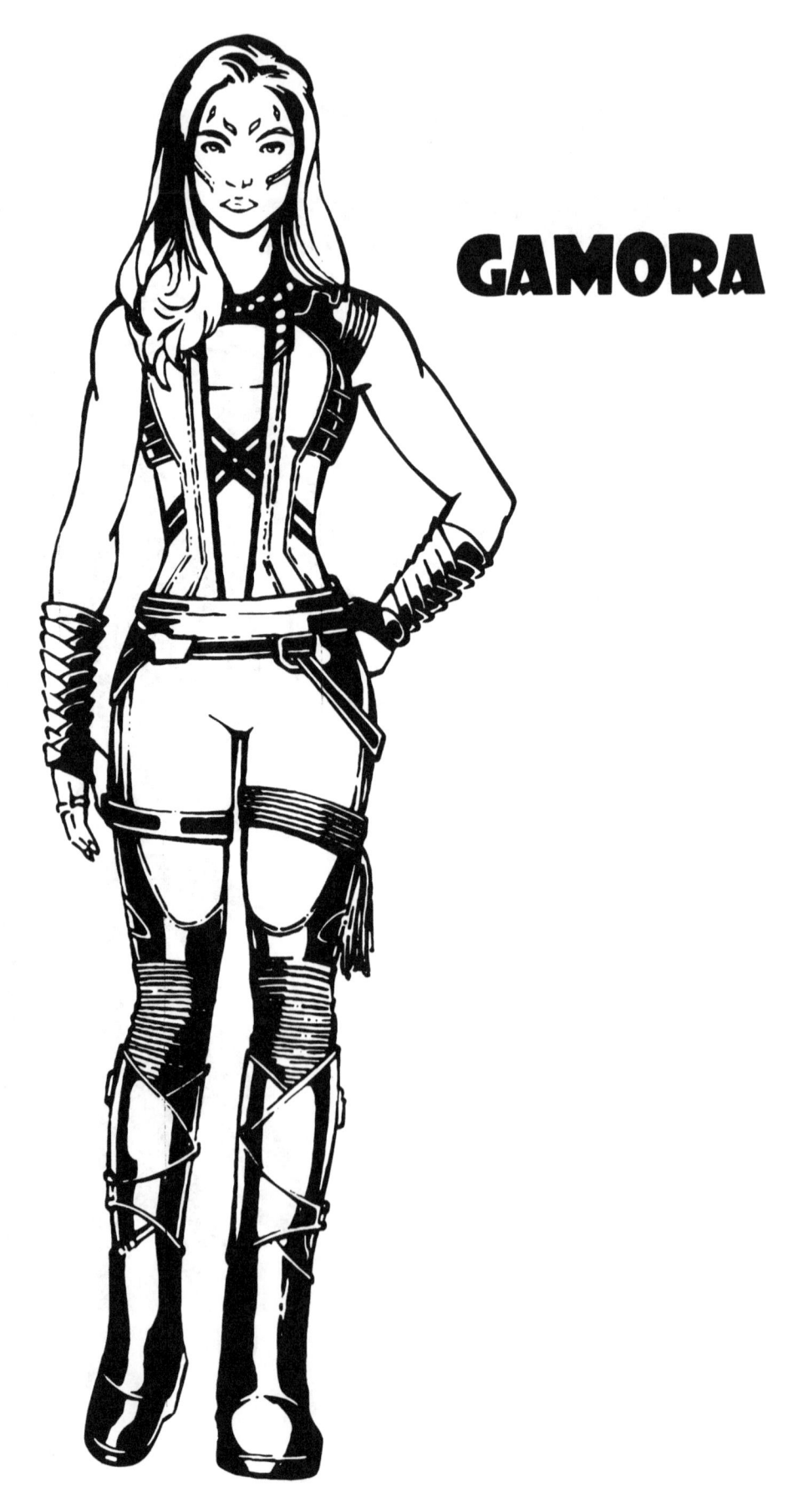

GAMORA

NIGHTWING

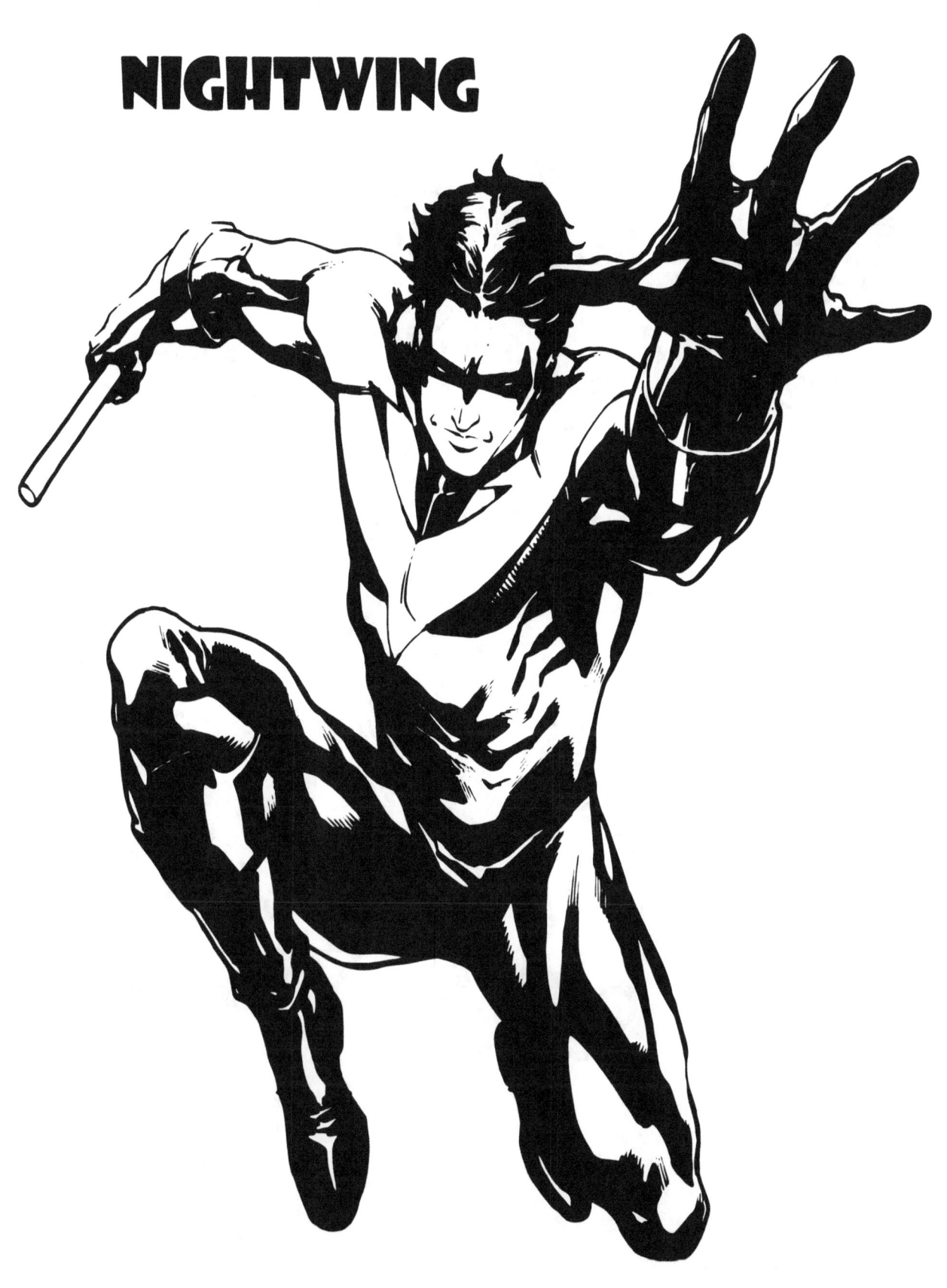

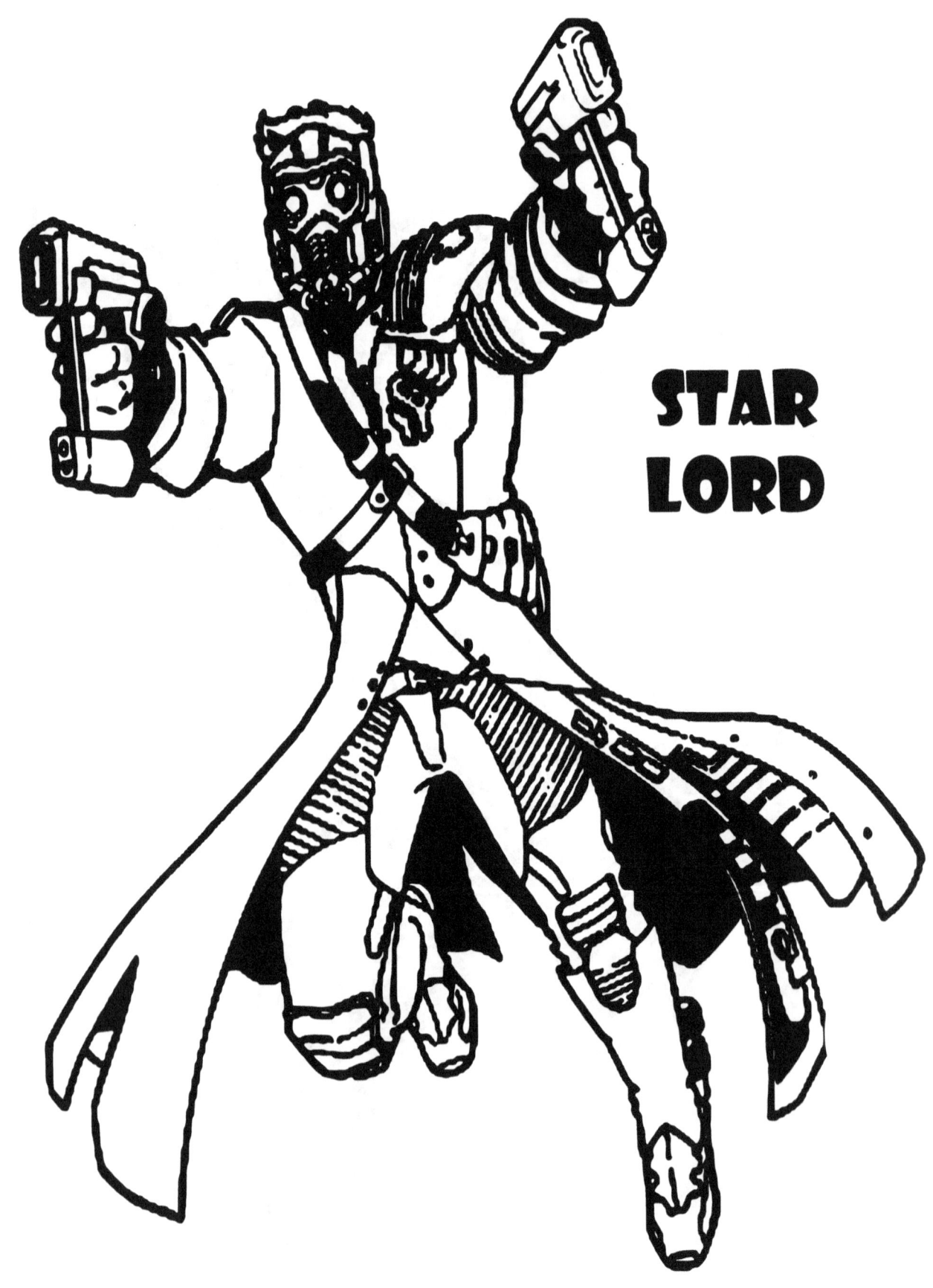

STAR
LORD

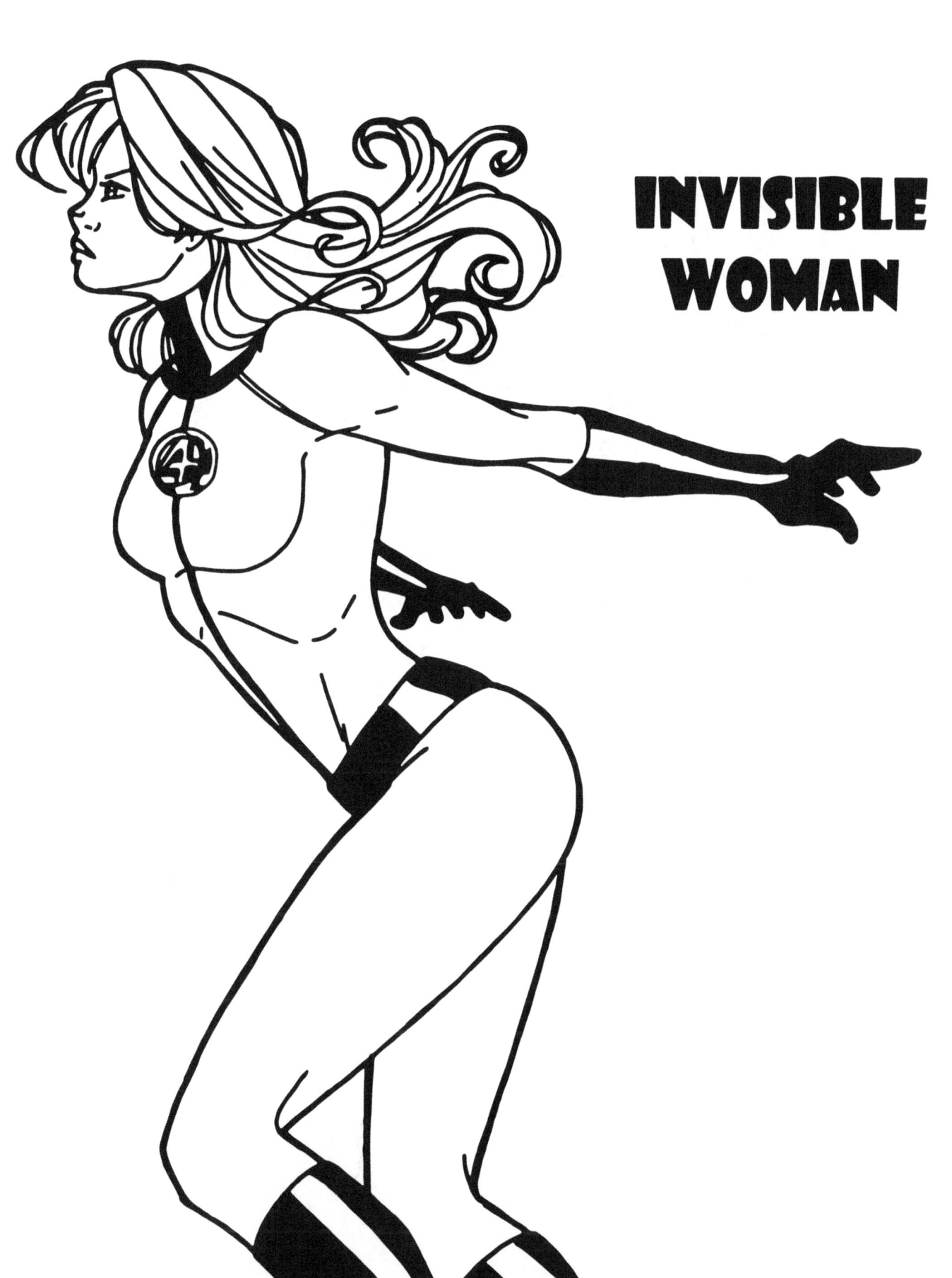

INVISIBLE WOMAN

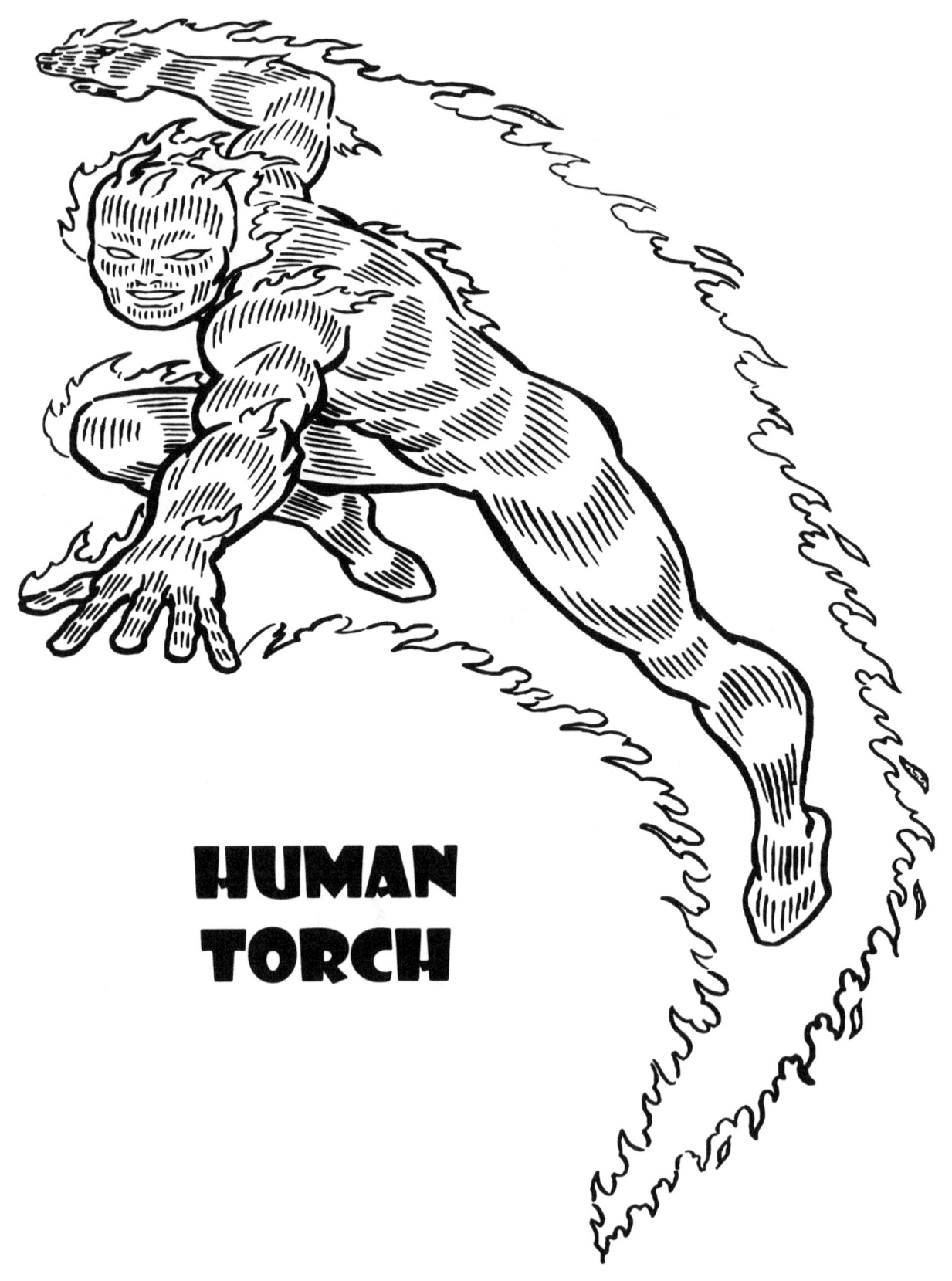

HUMAN TORCH

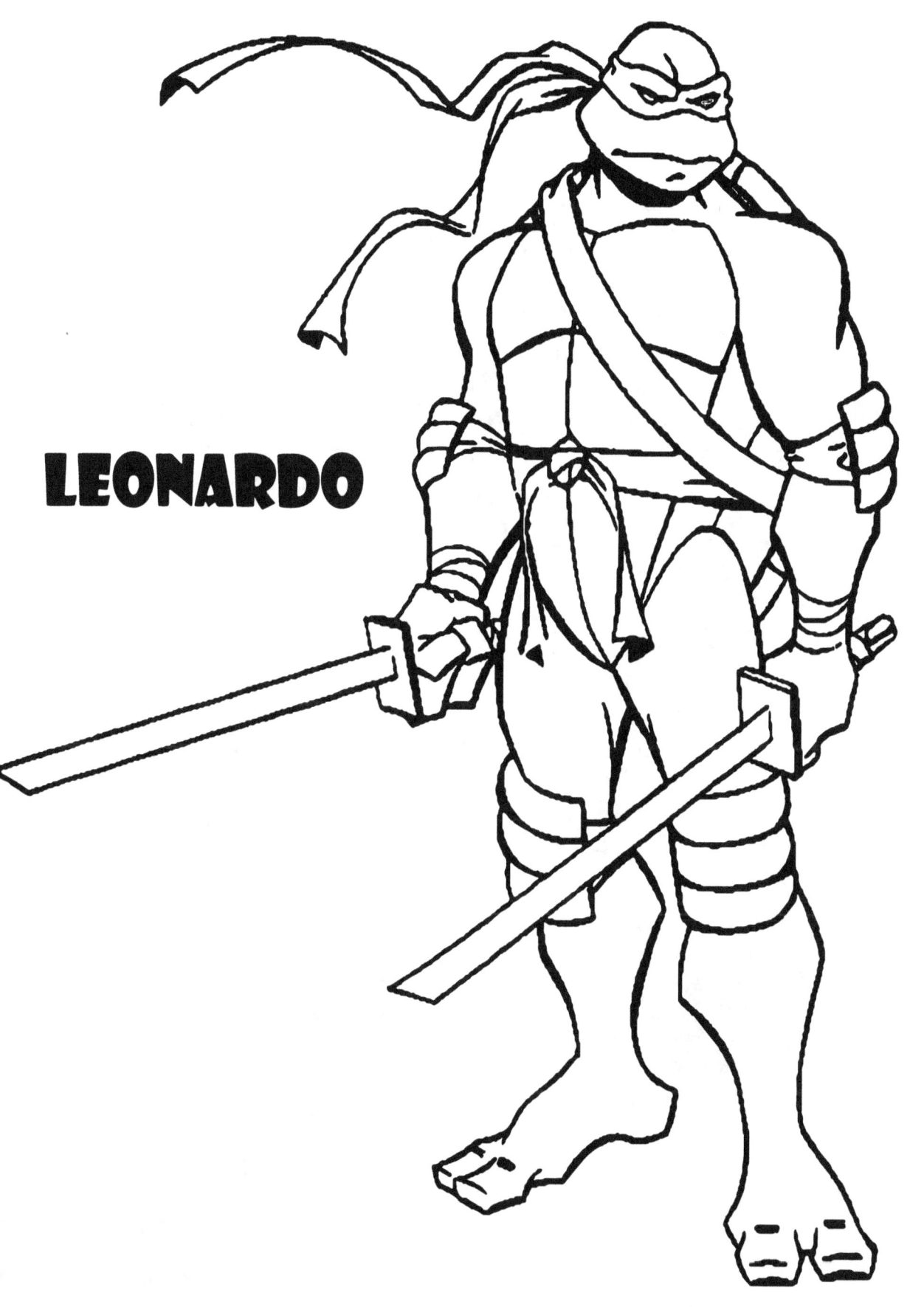

LEONARDO

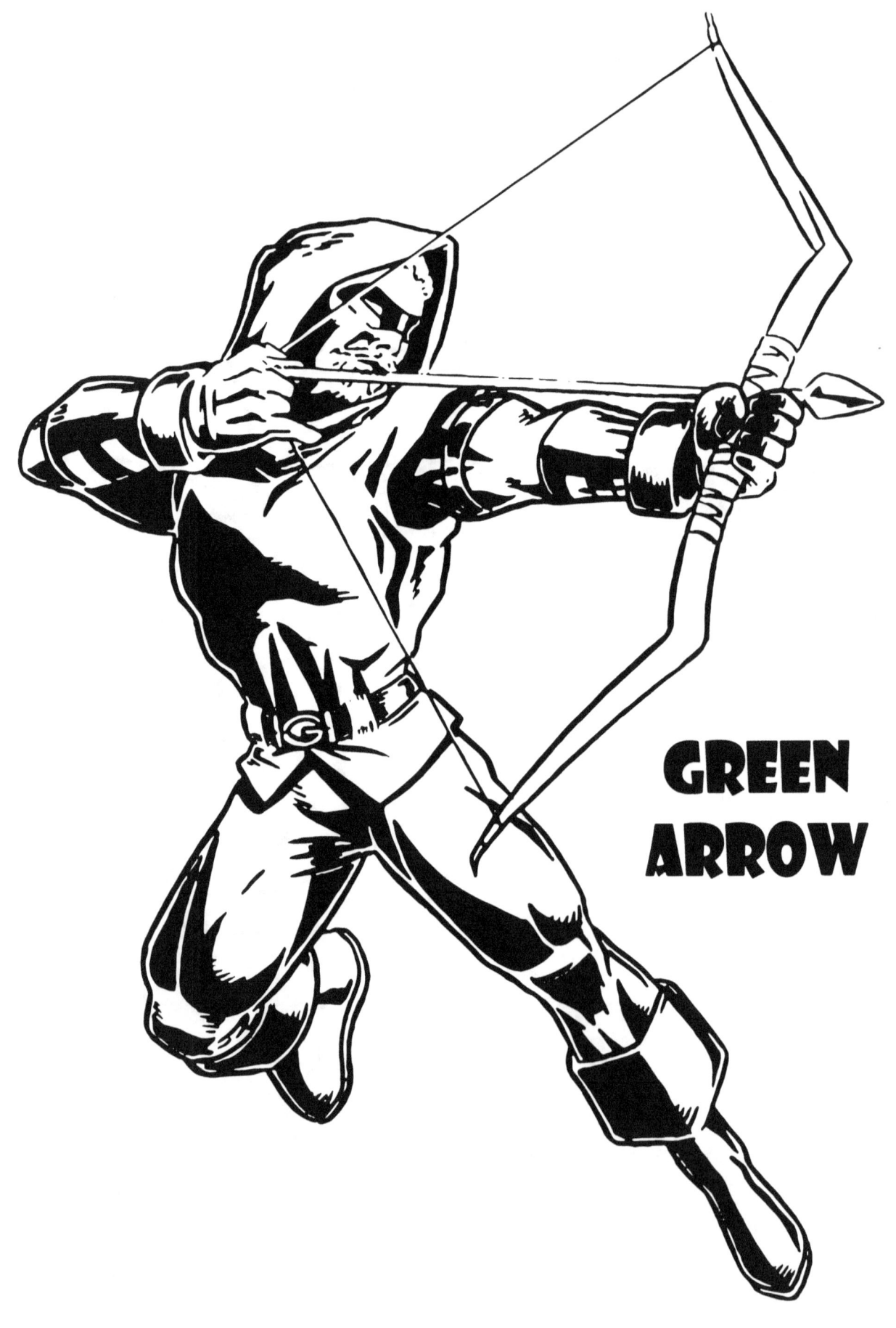

GREEN
ARROW

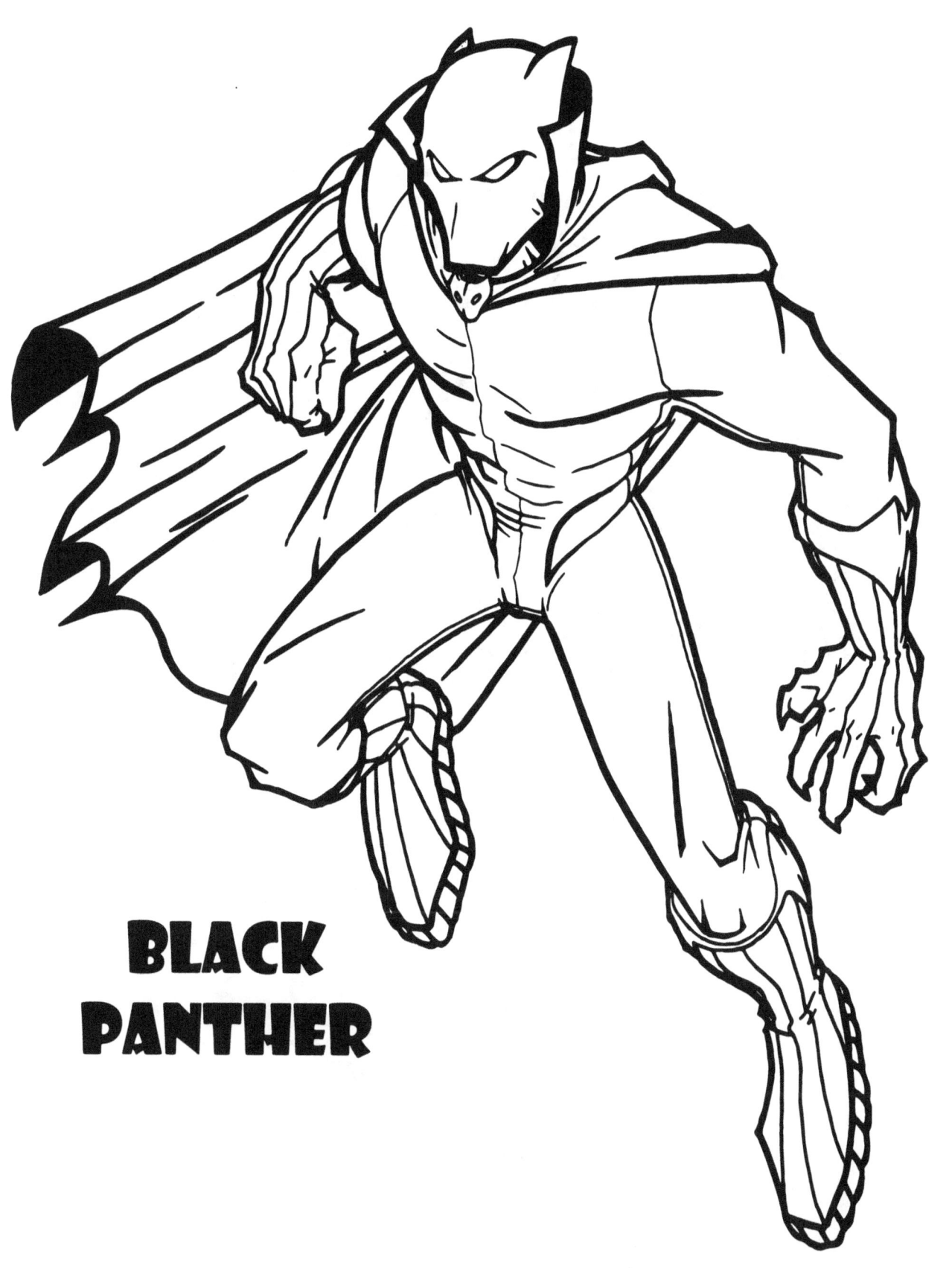

BLACK
PANTHER

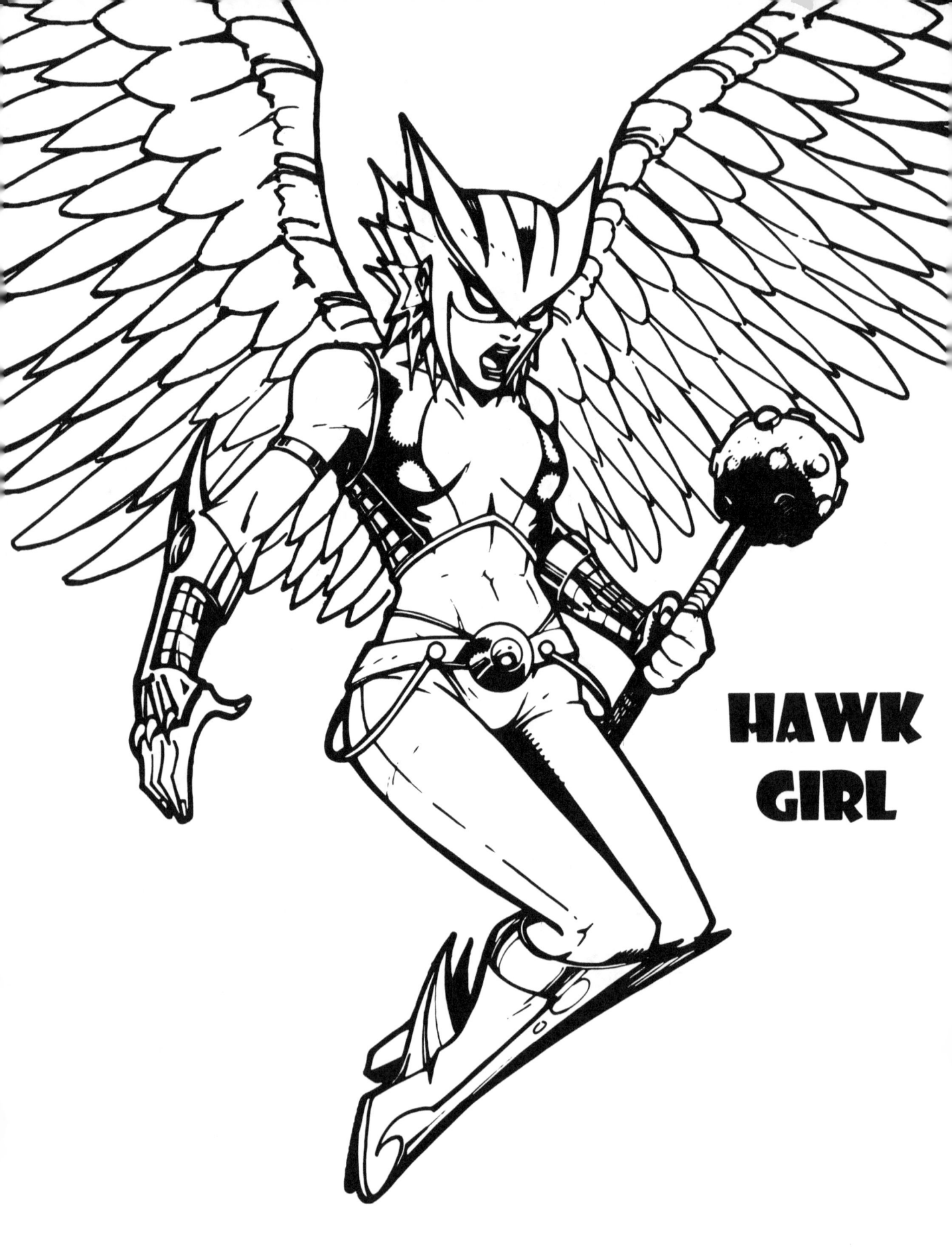

HAWK GIRL

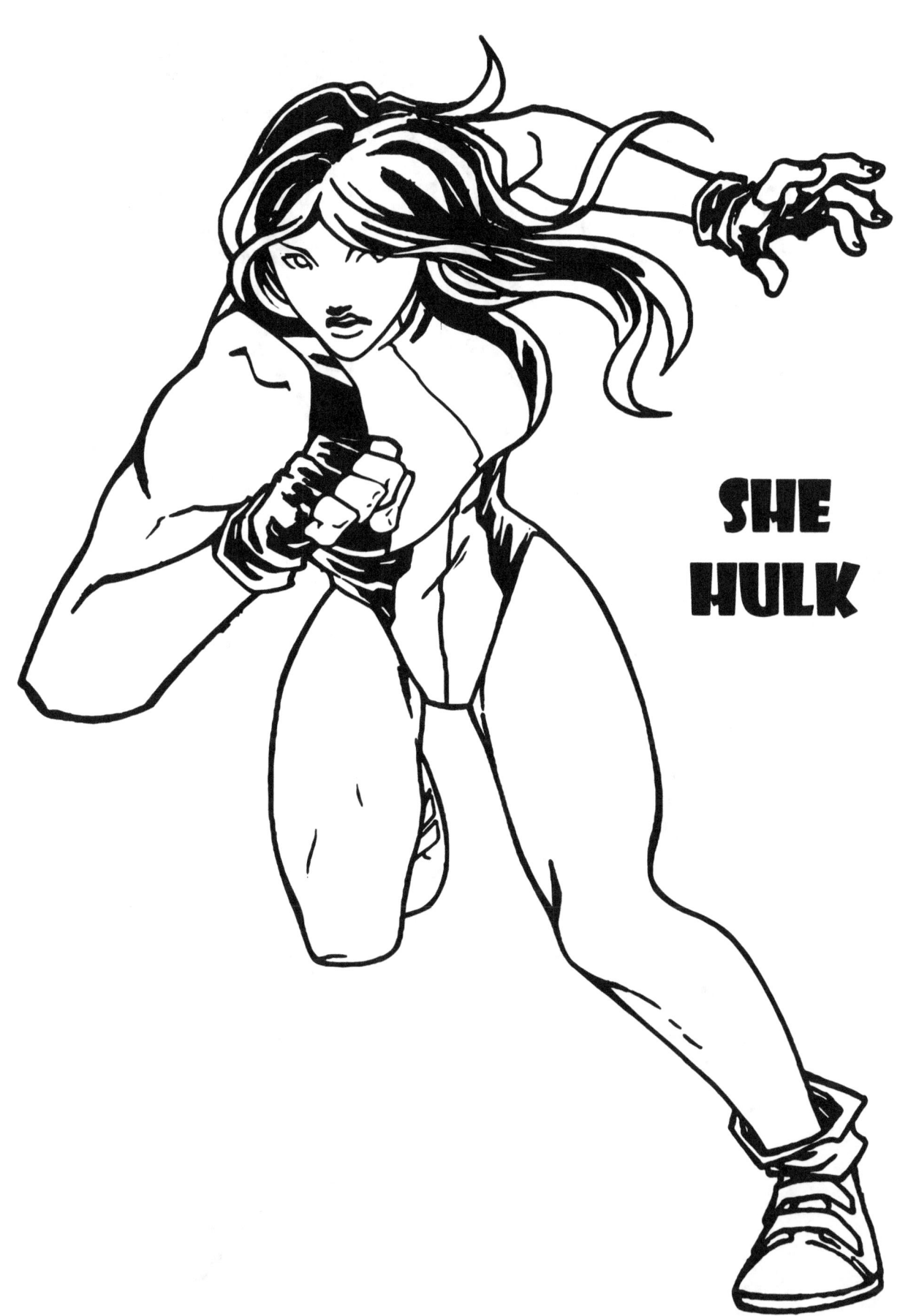

SHE
HULK

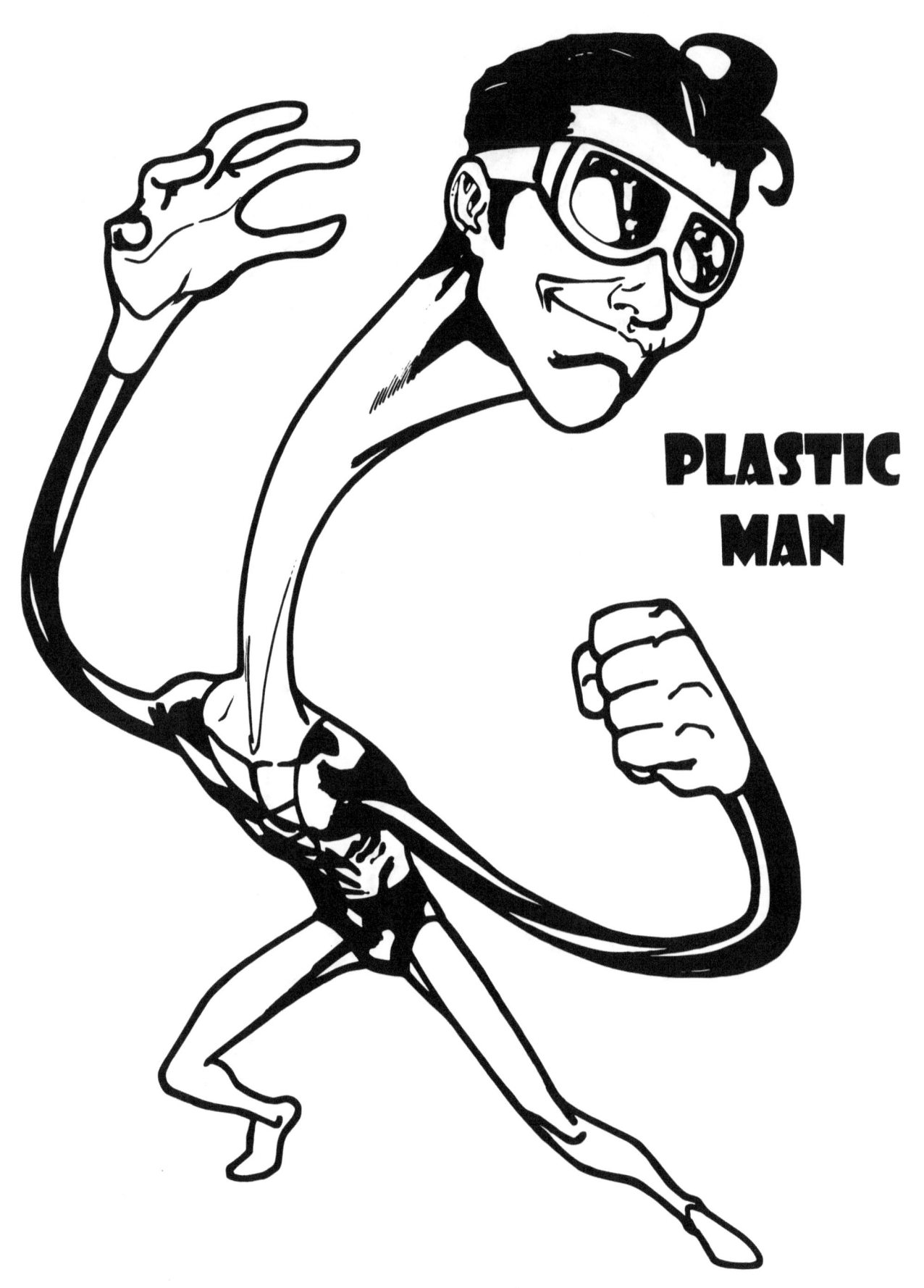

PLASTIC
MAN

STORM

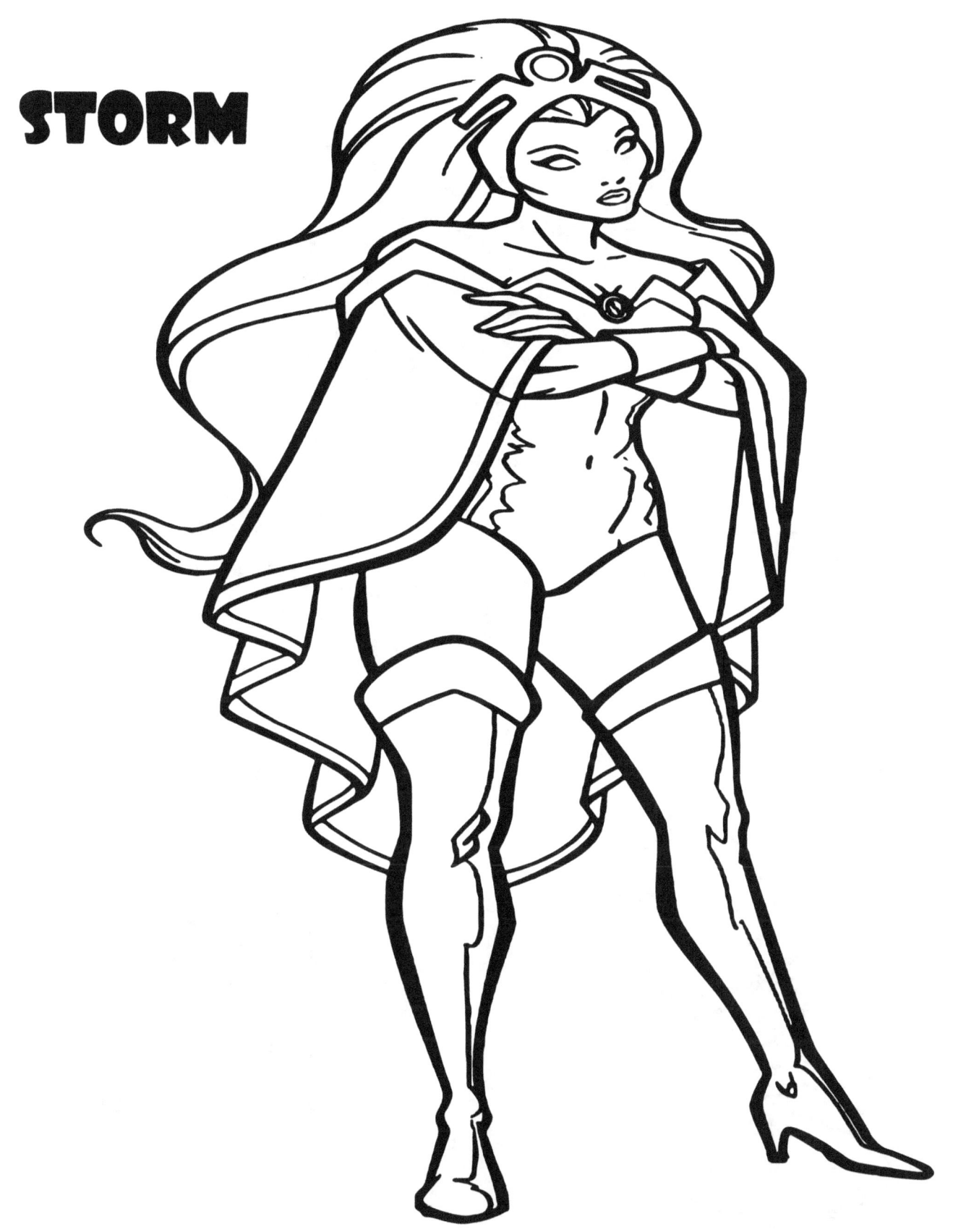

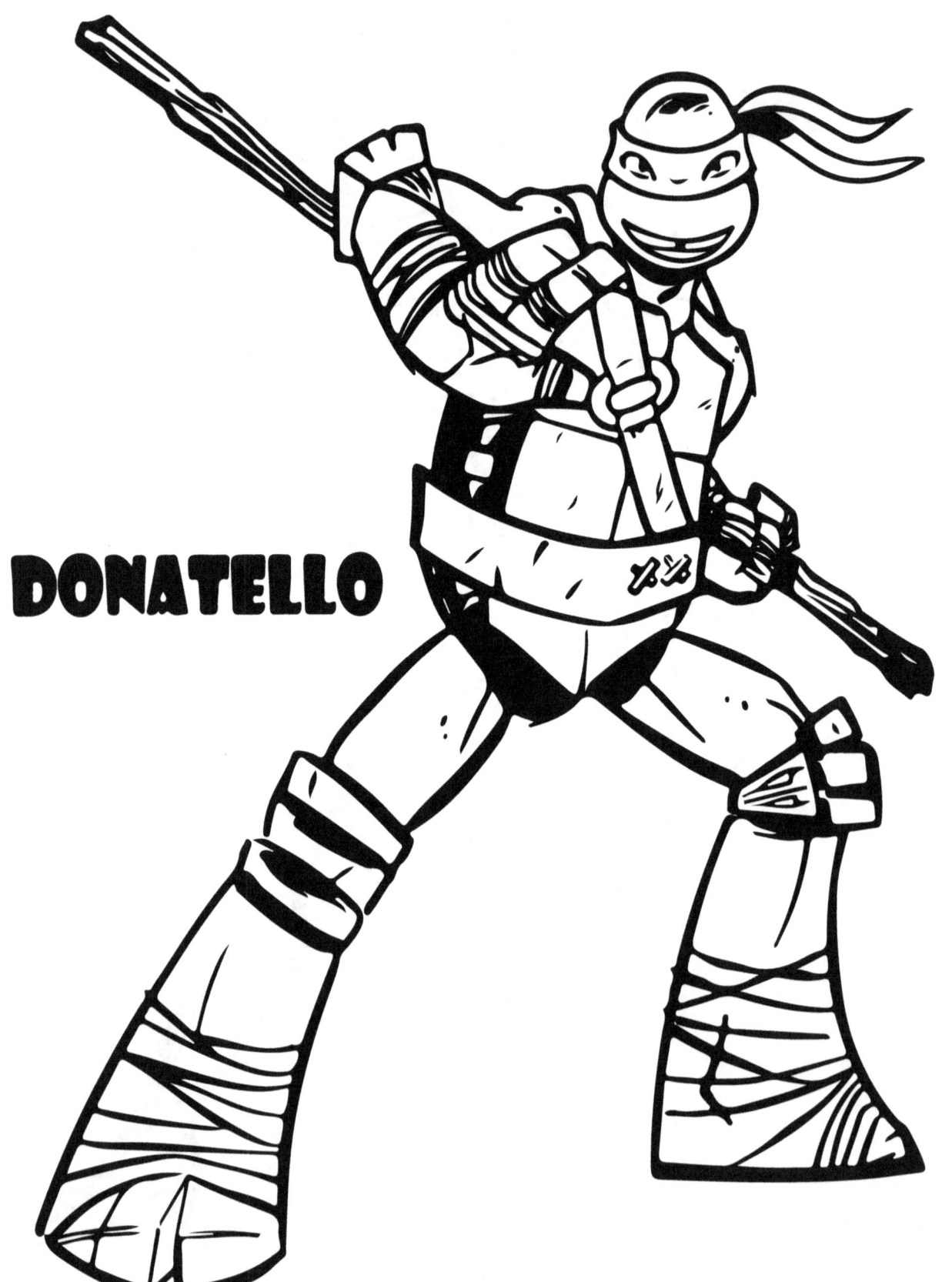

DONATELLO

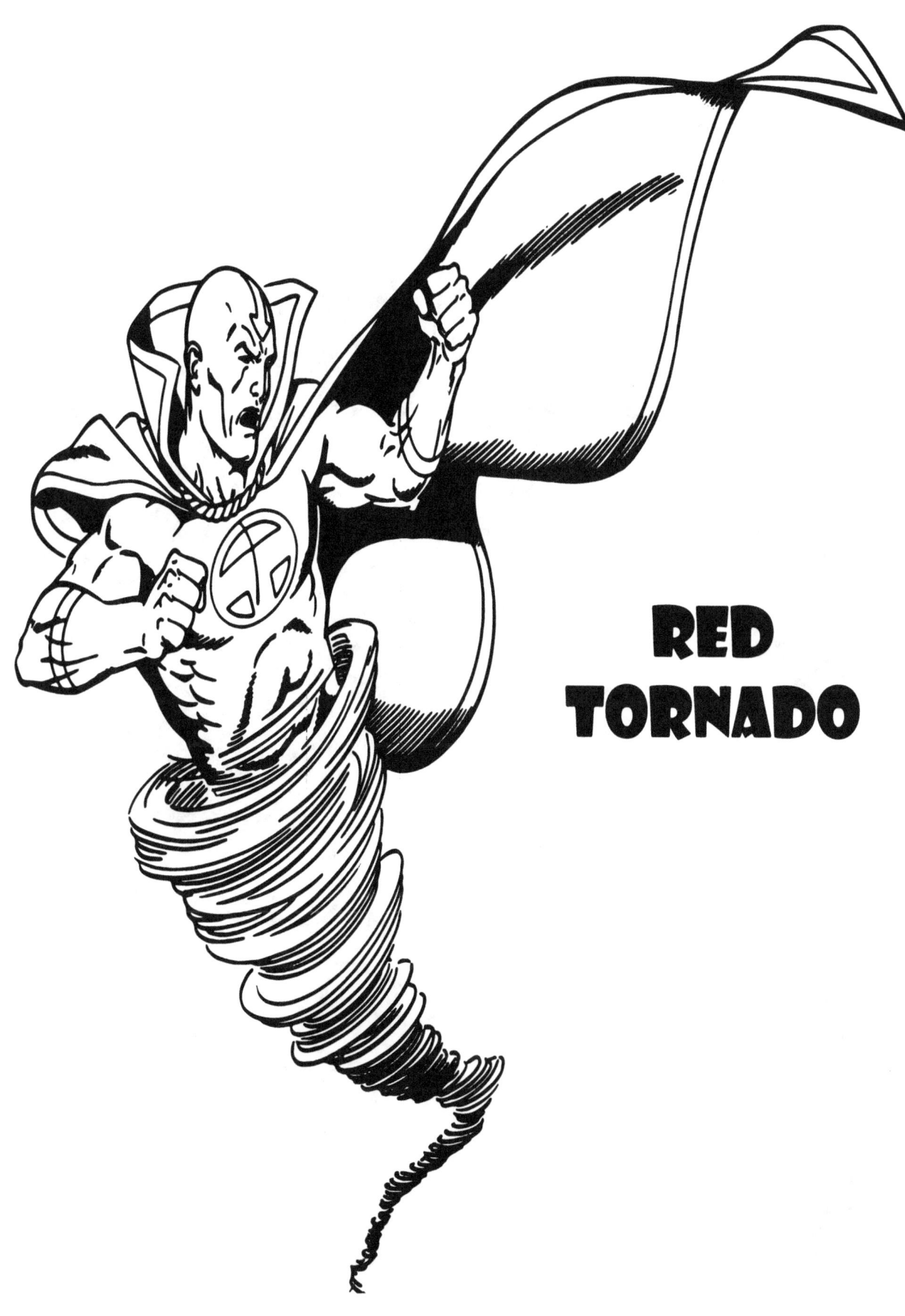

RED
TORNADO

BLUE BEETLE

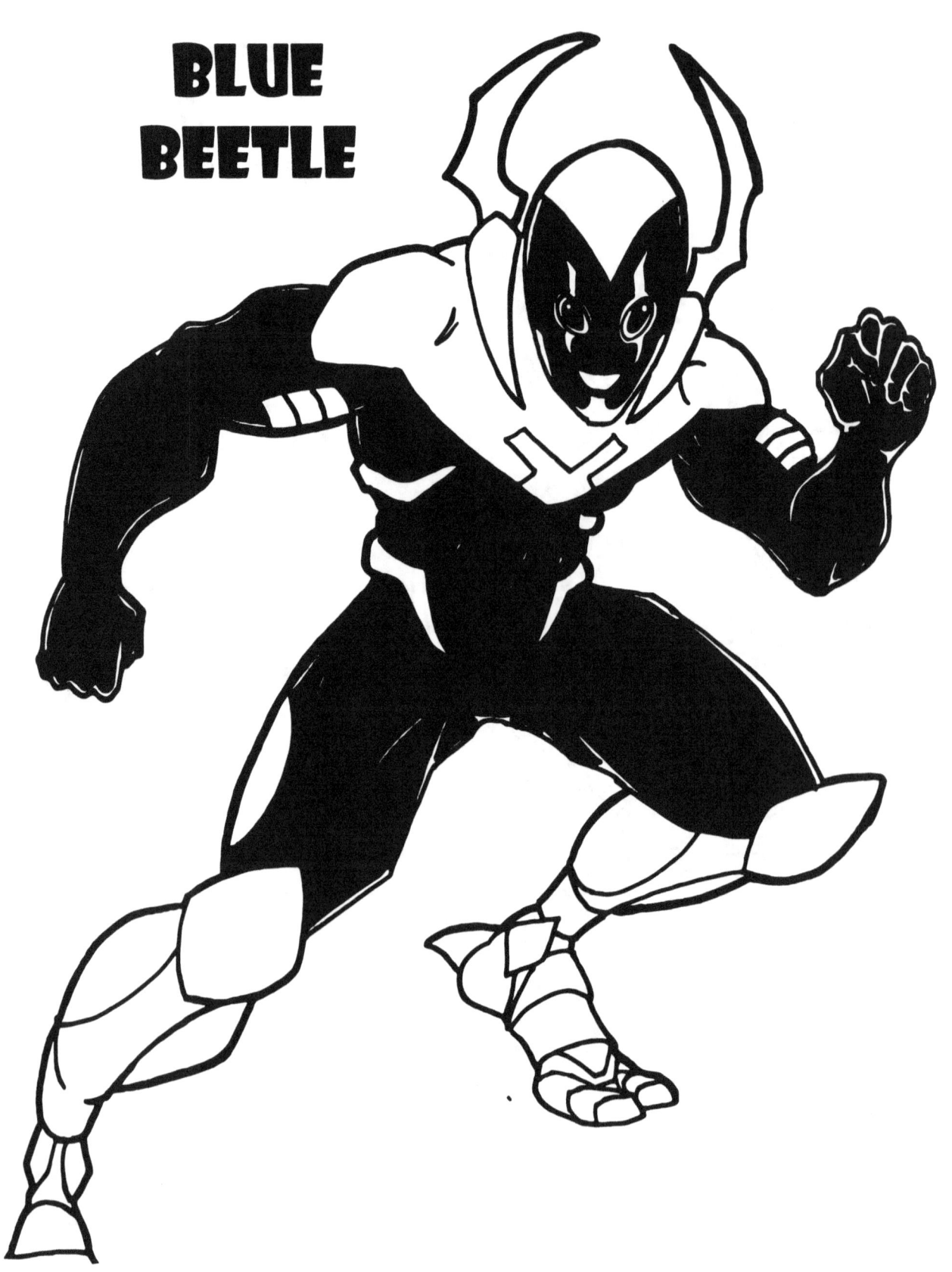

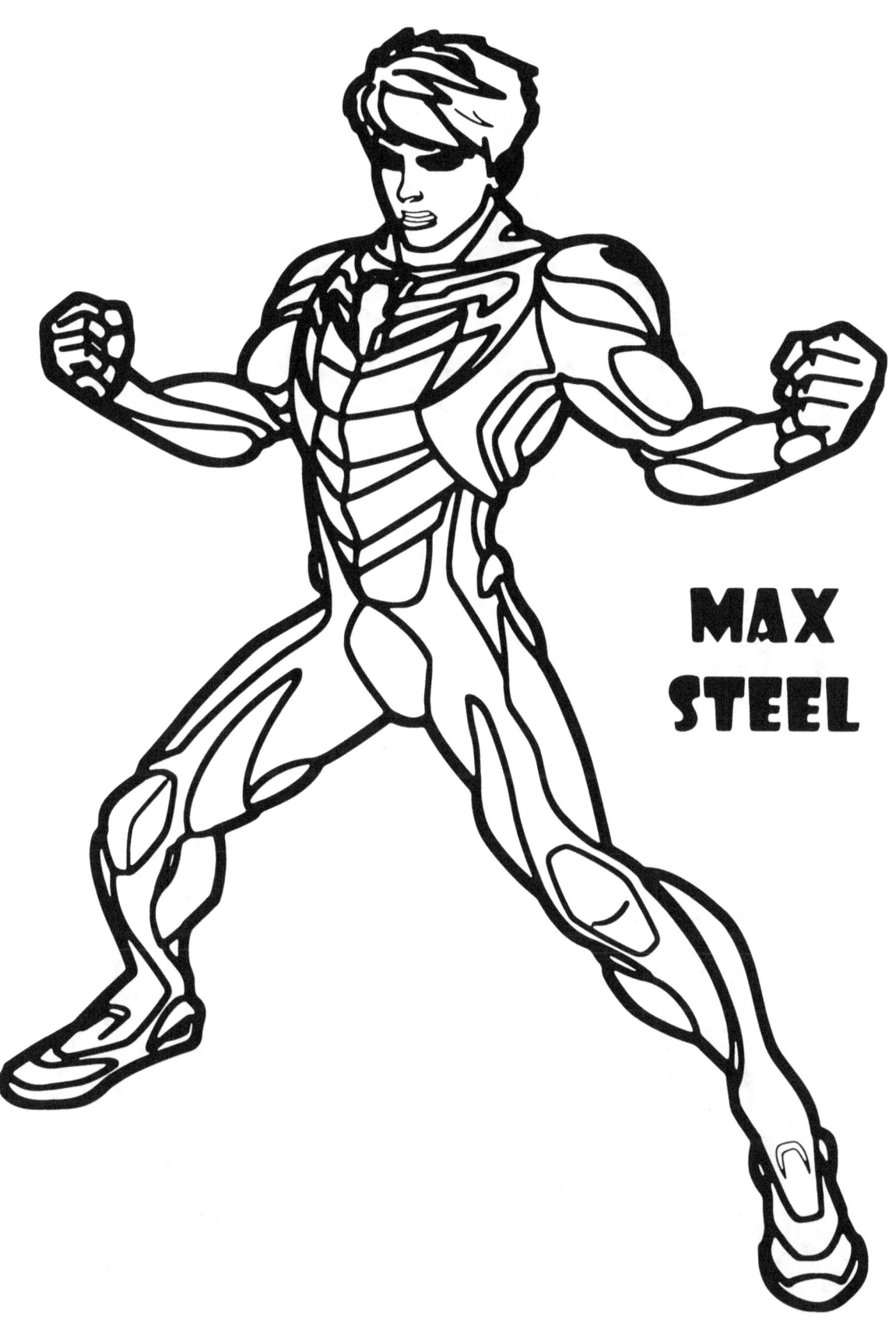

MAX
STEEL

BUMBLEBEE

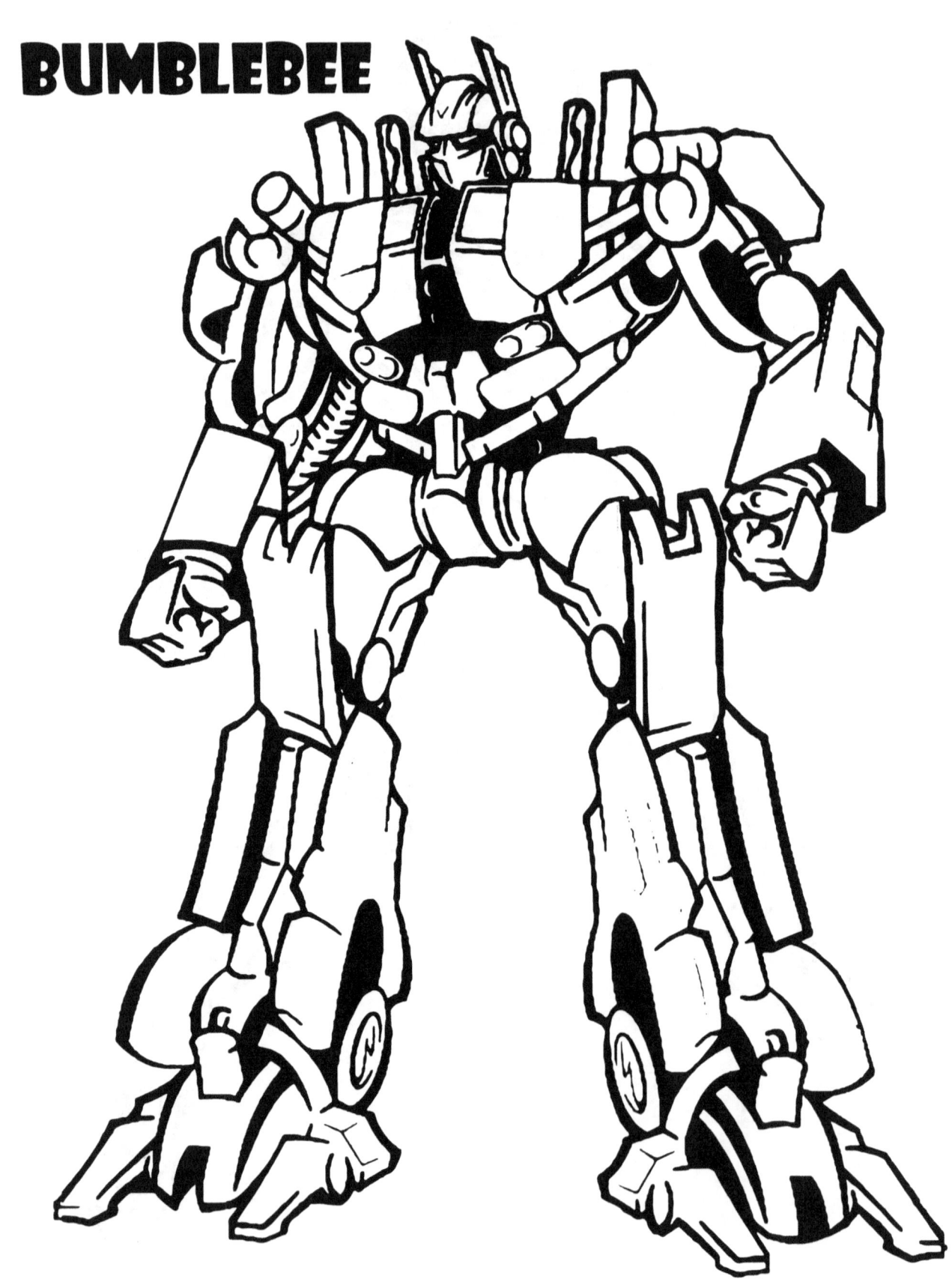

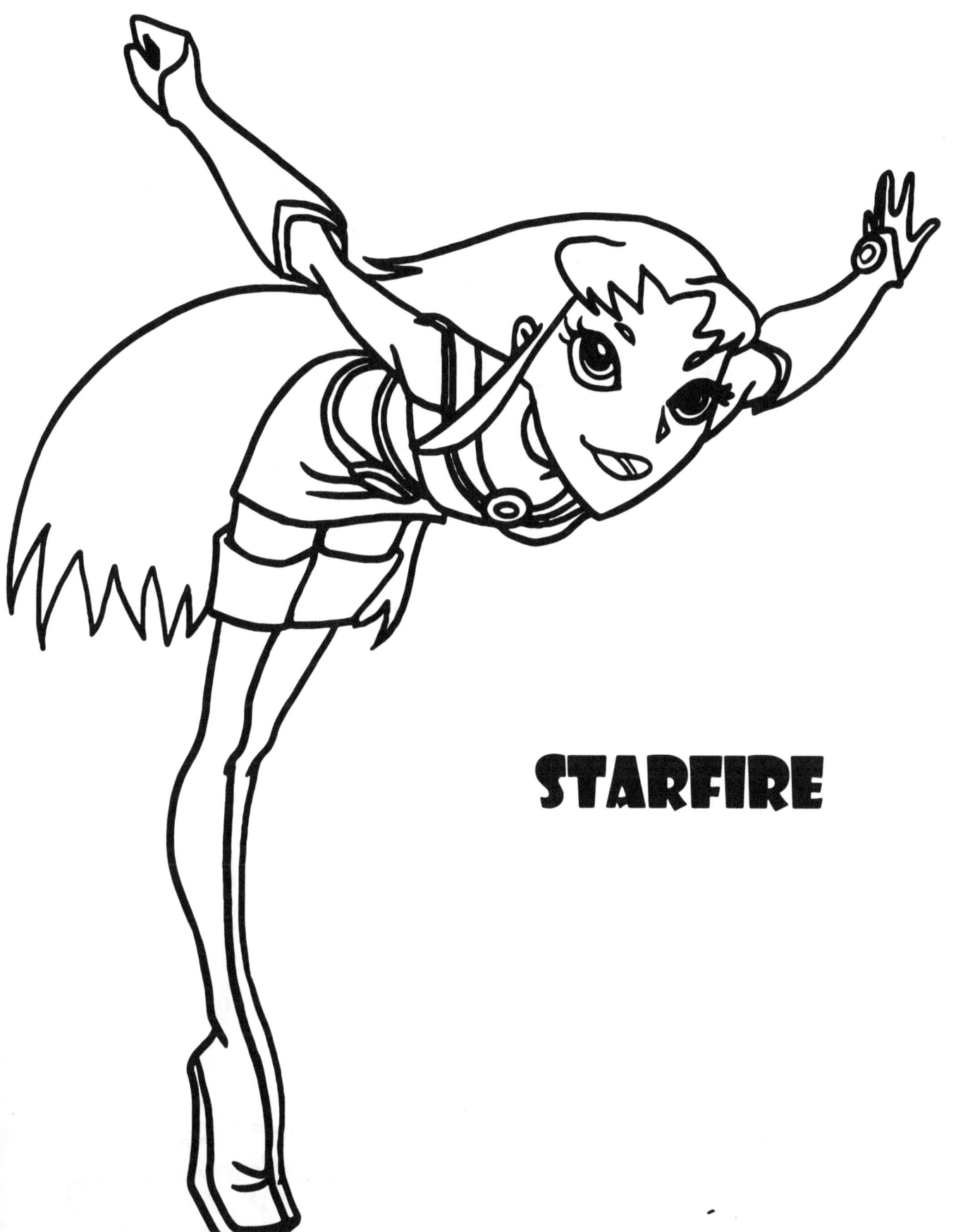

STARFIRE

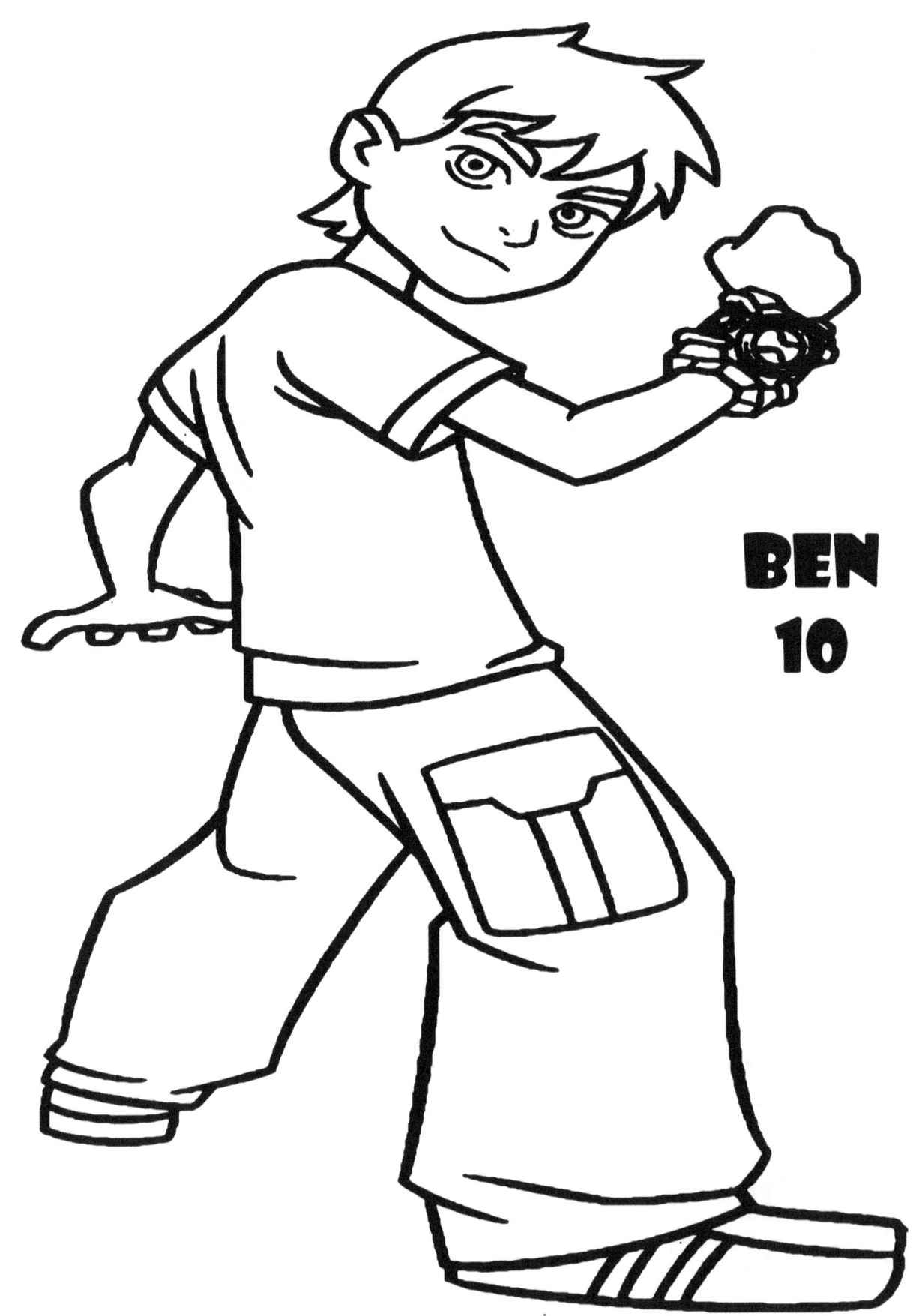

WYLDSTYLE

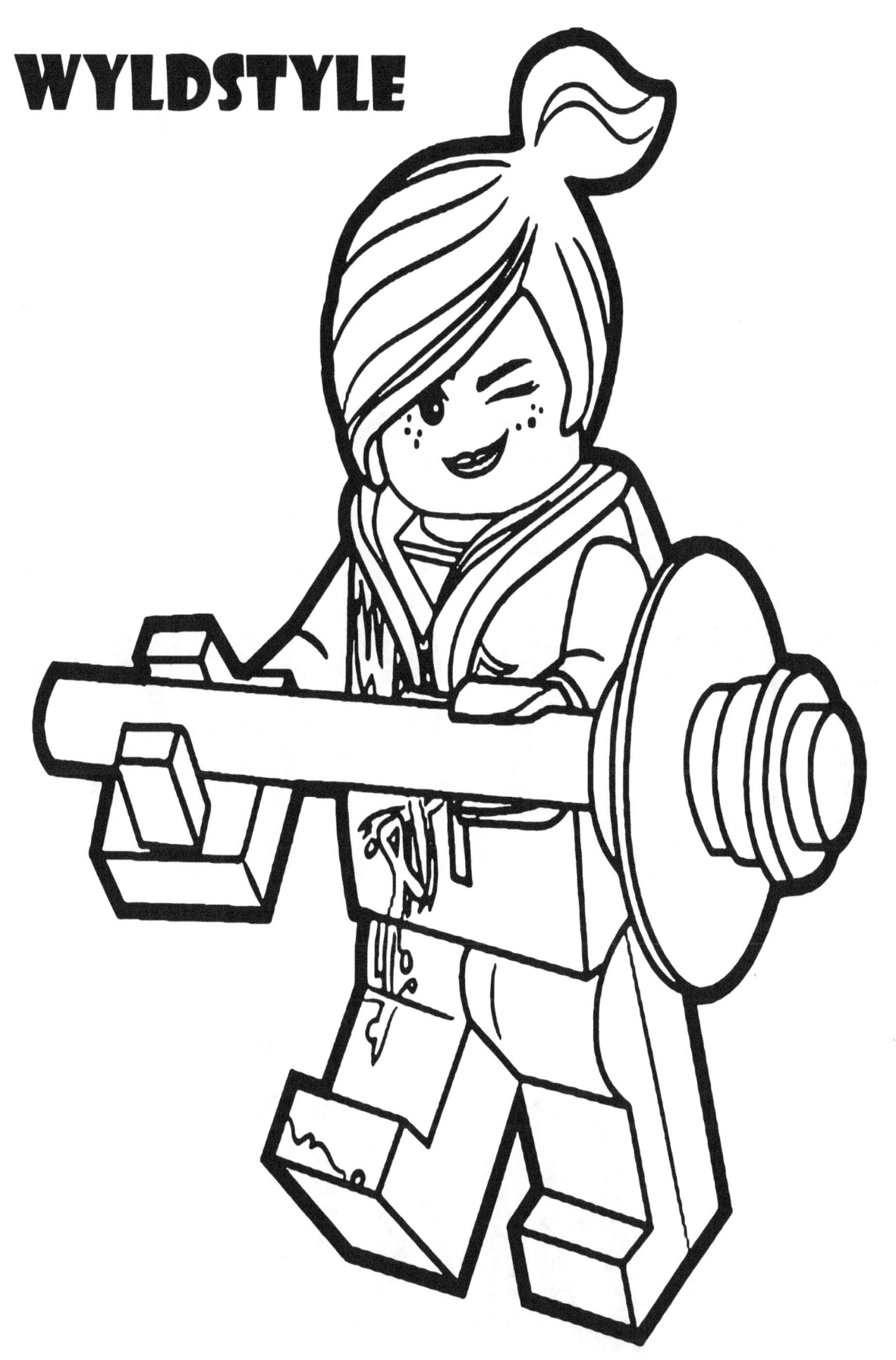

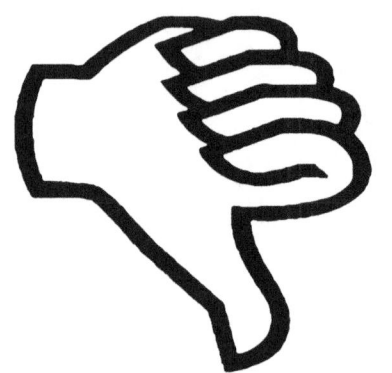

HISS

VILLAINS

Boo!

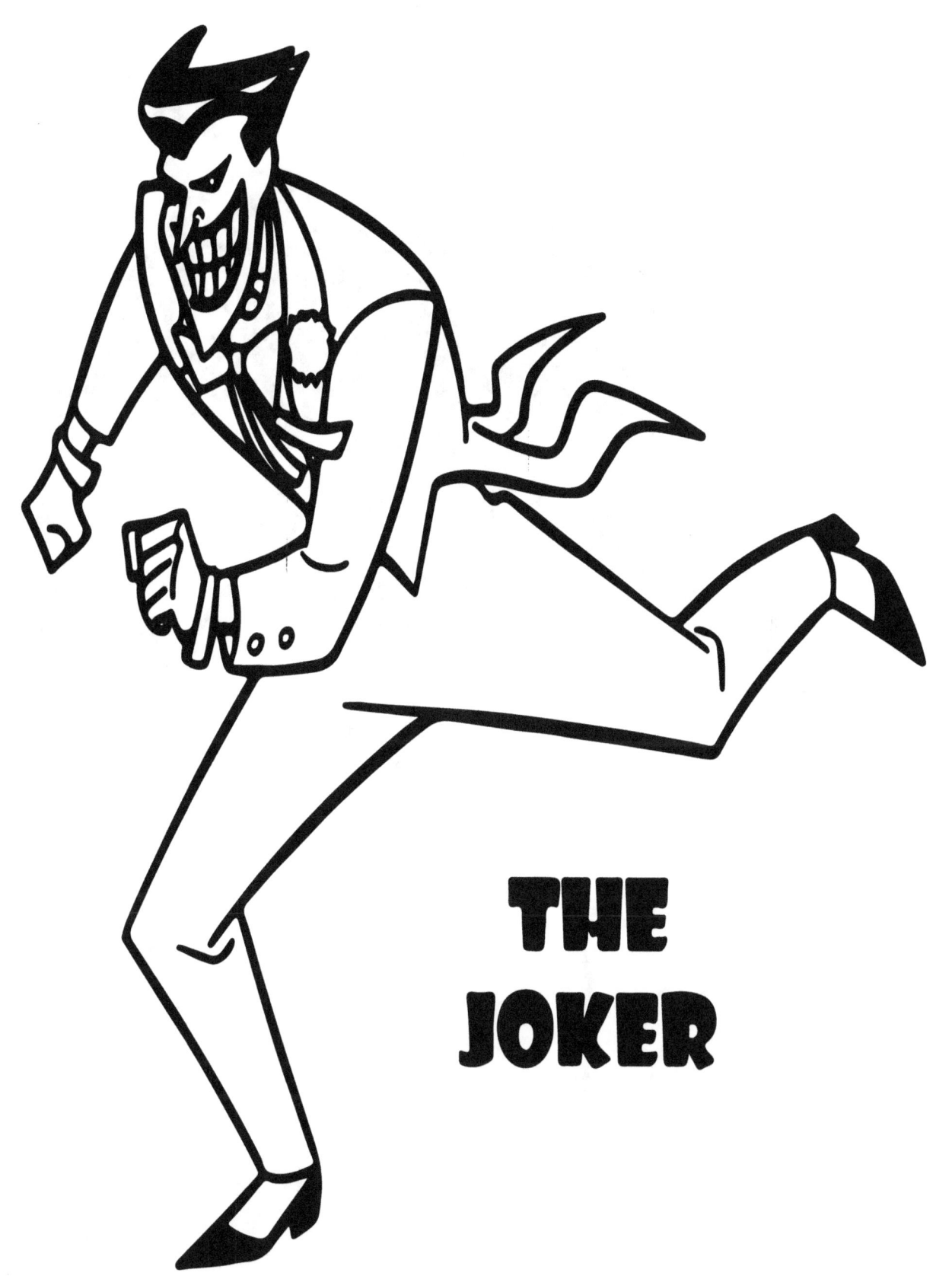

THE
JOKER

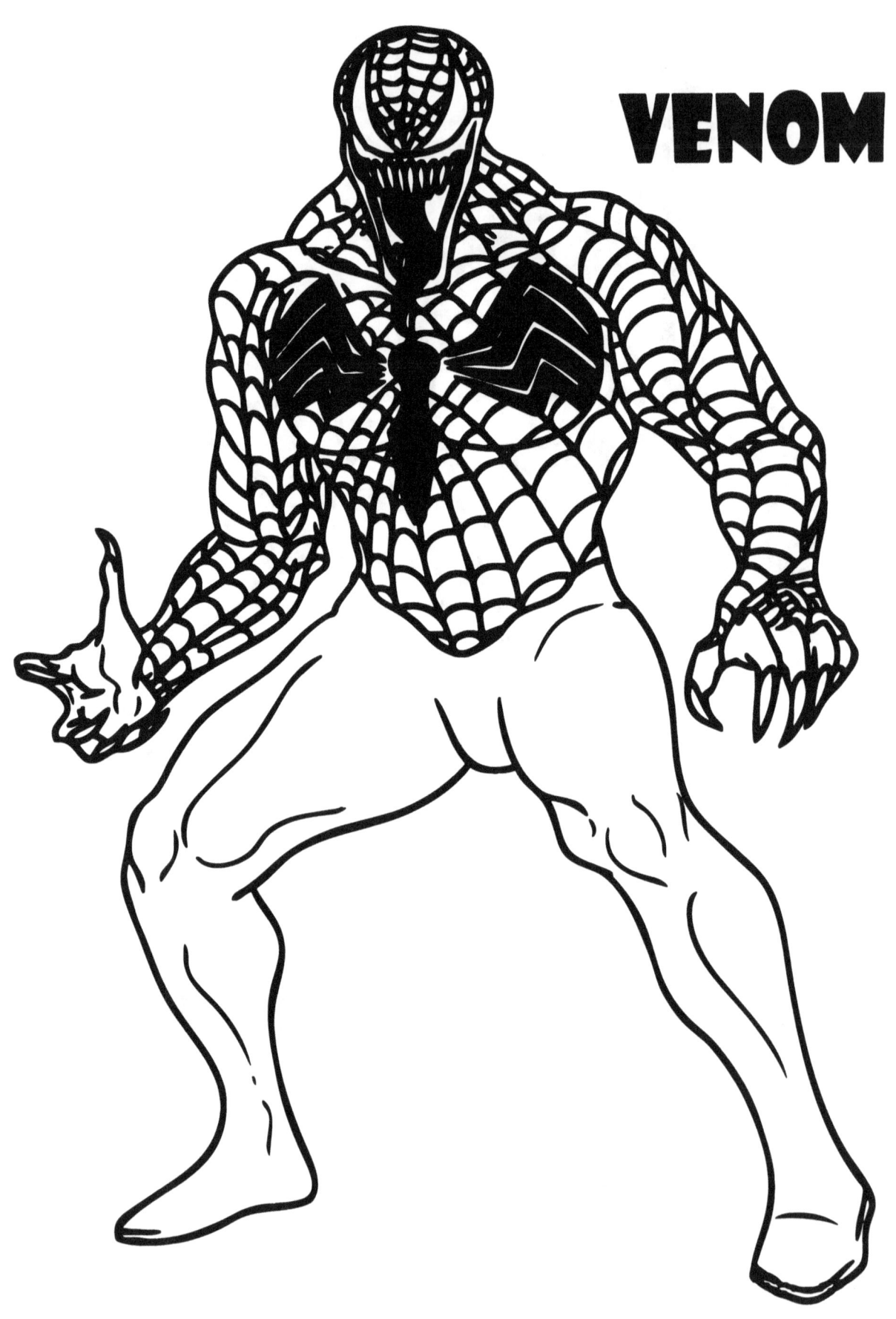

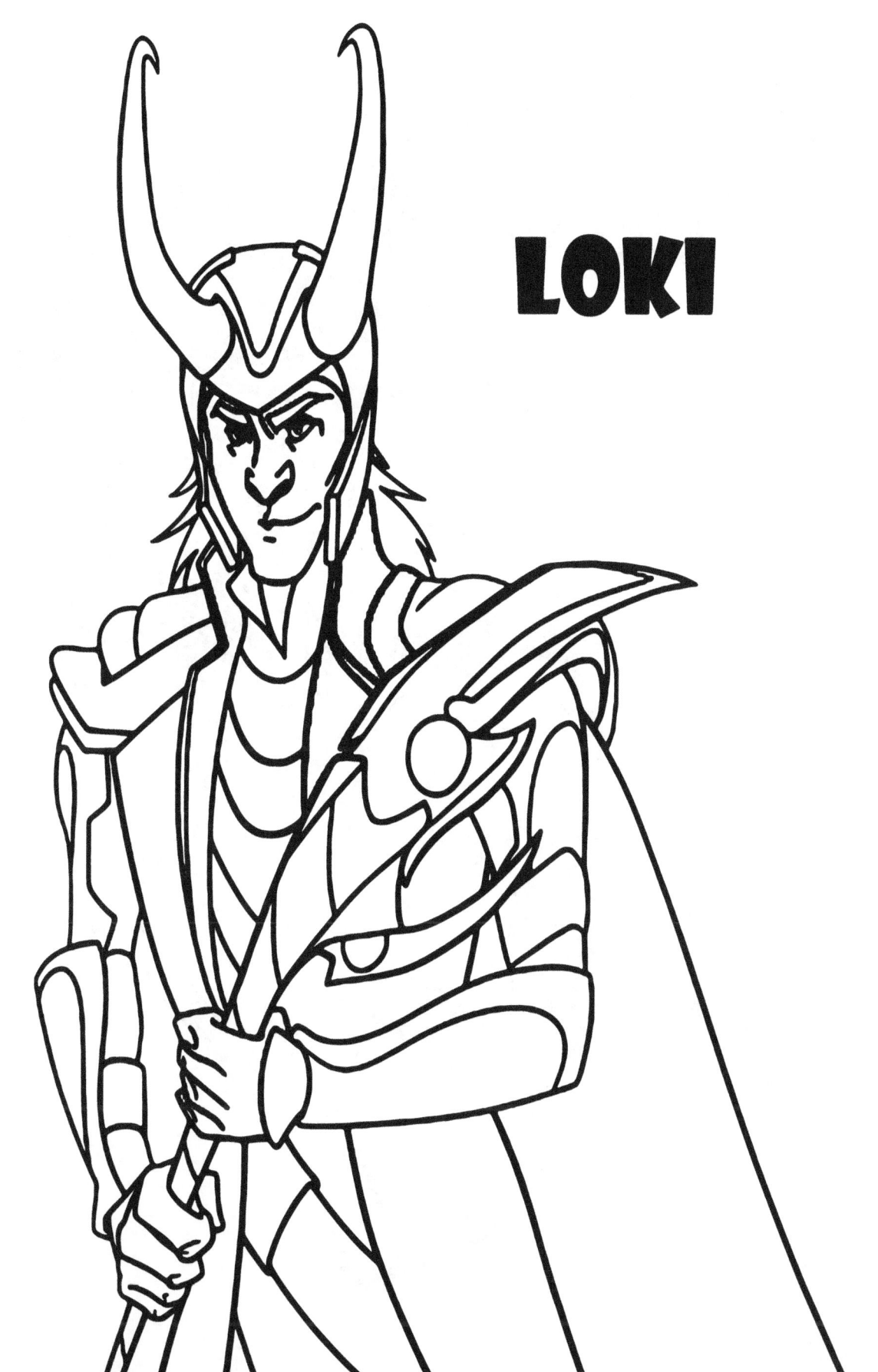

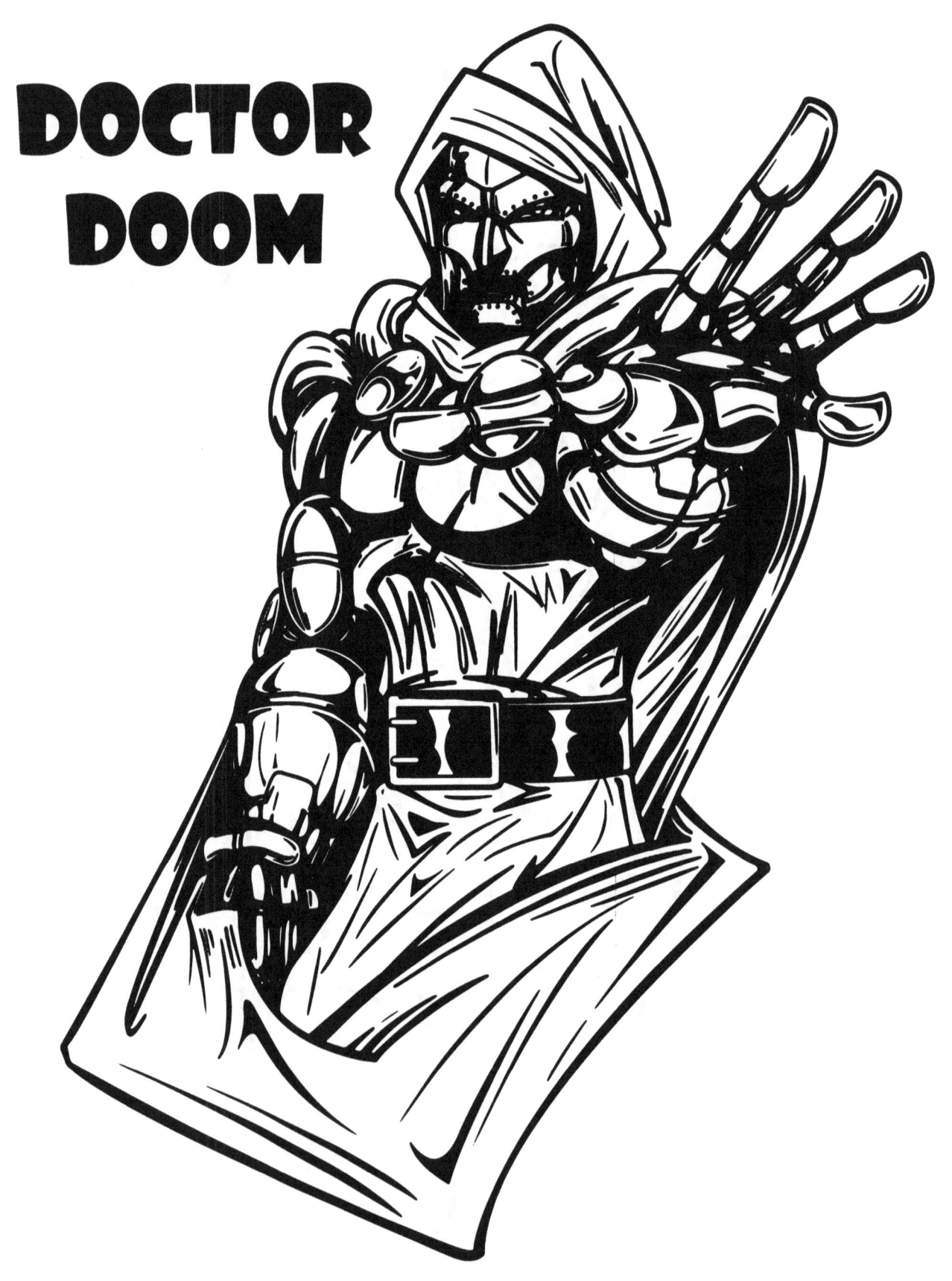

DOCTOR
DOOM

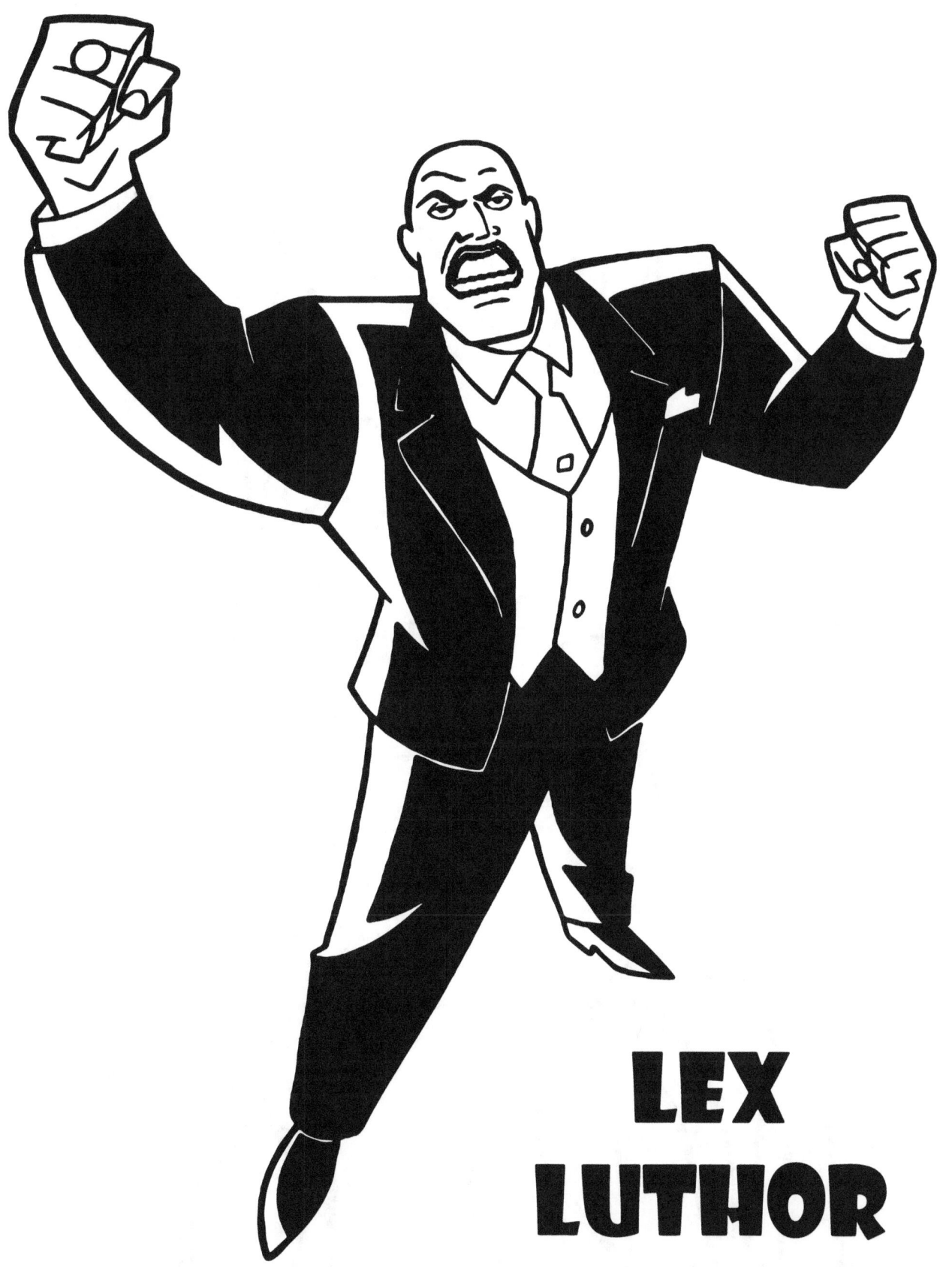

LEX
LUTHOR

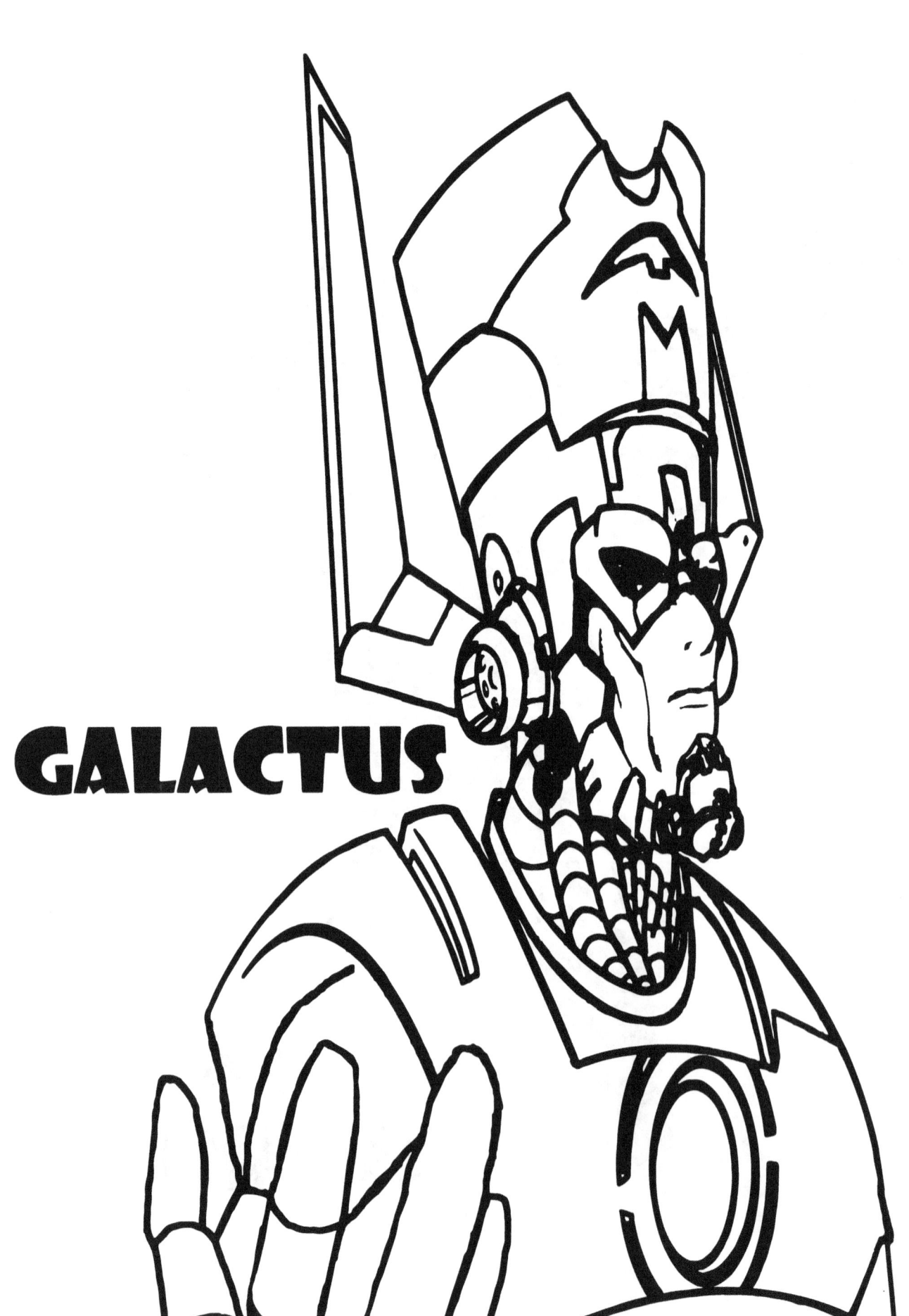

GALACTUS

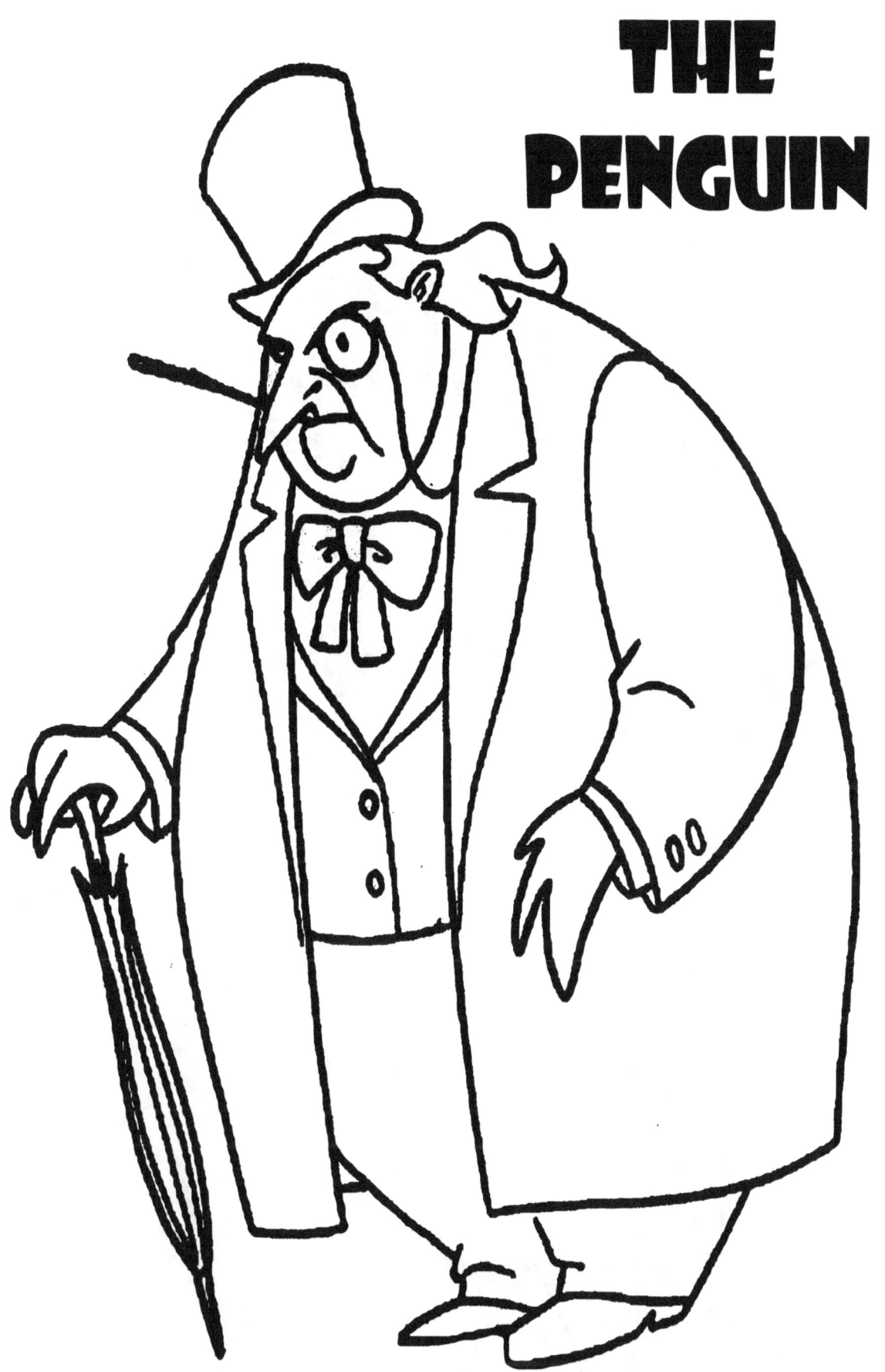

THE
PENGUIN

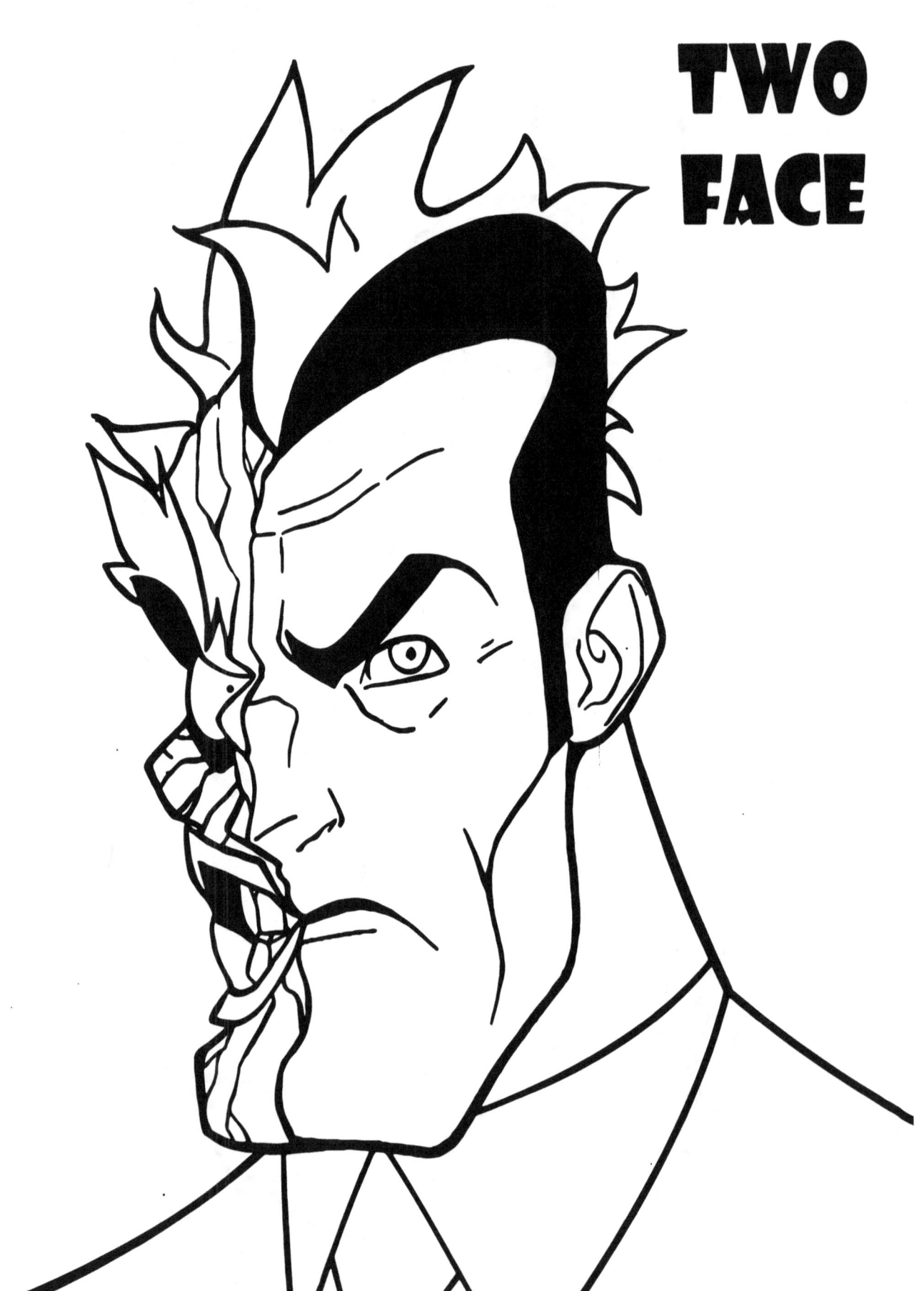

TWO
FACE

GREEN GOBLIN

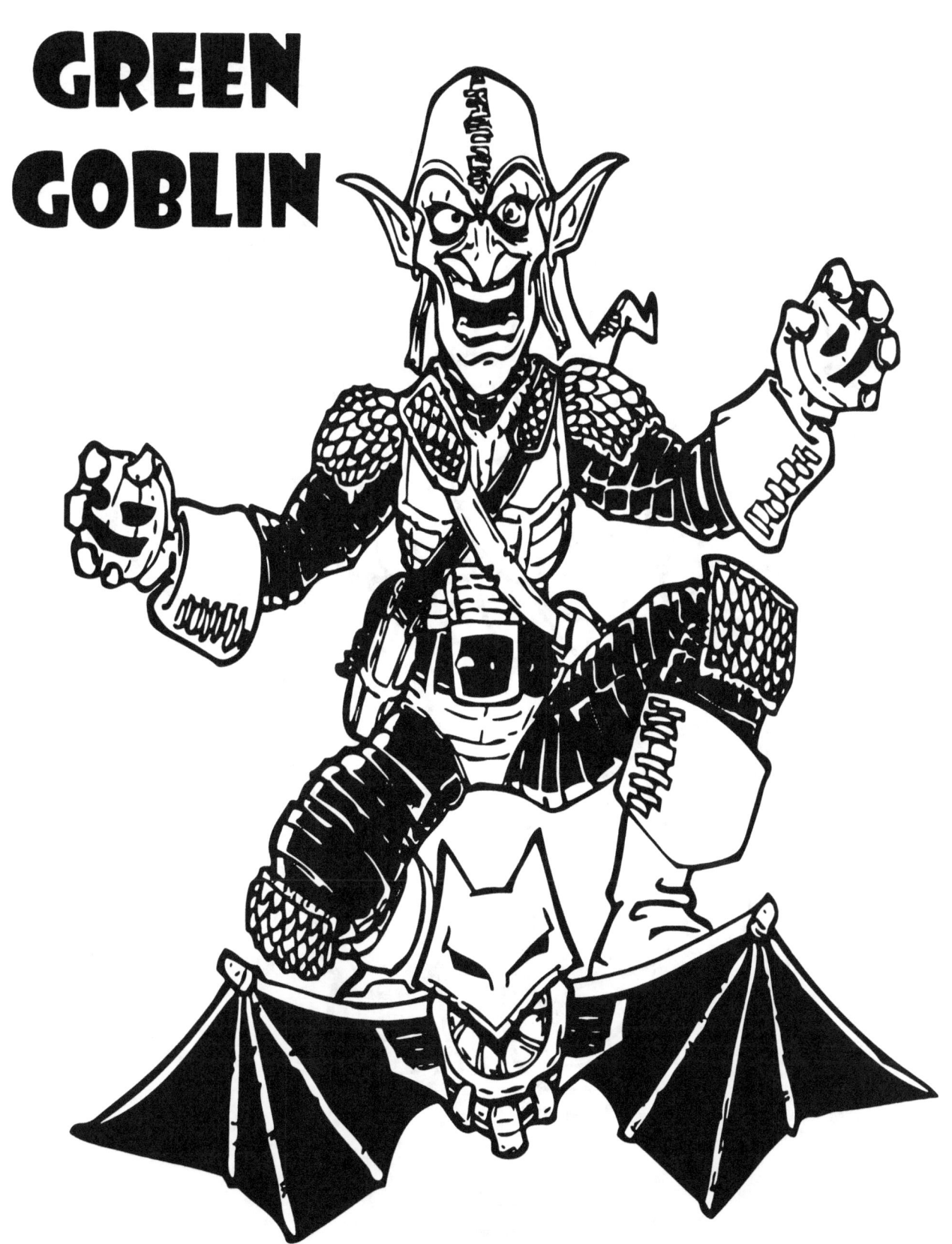

JUGGERNAUT

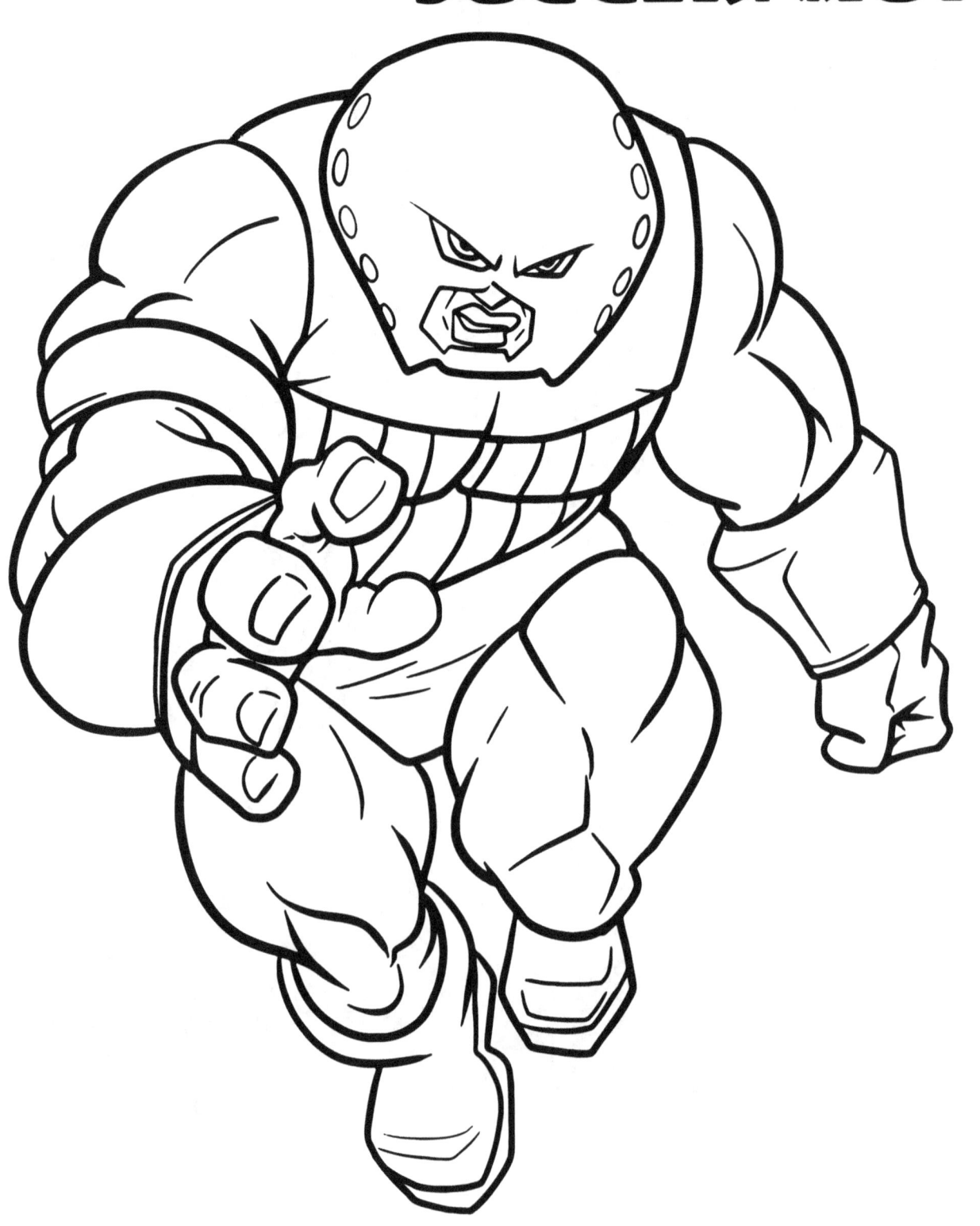

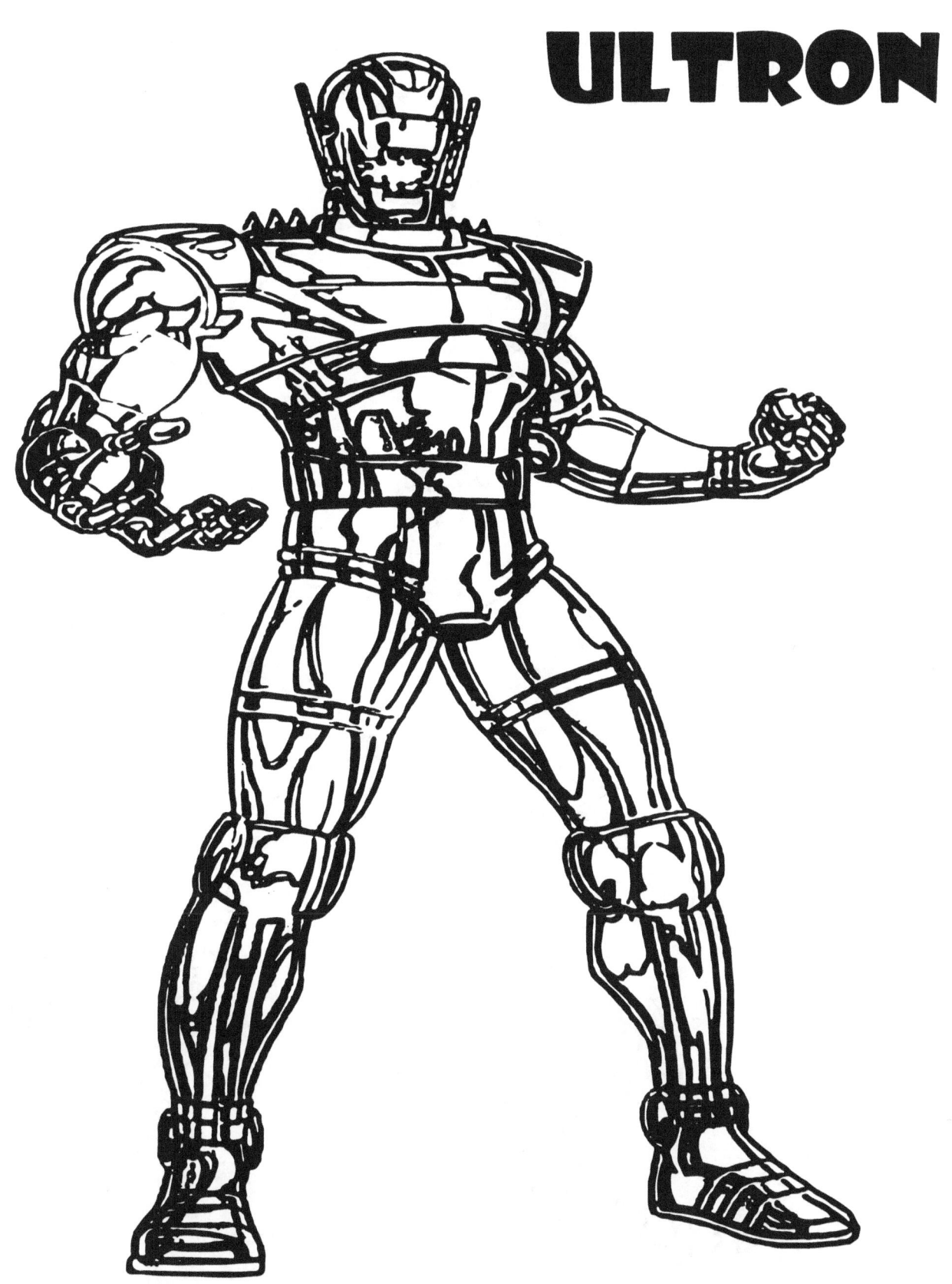

ULTRON

DOCTOR OCTOPUSS

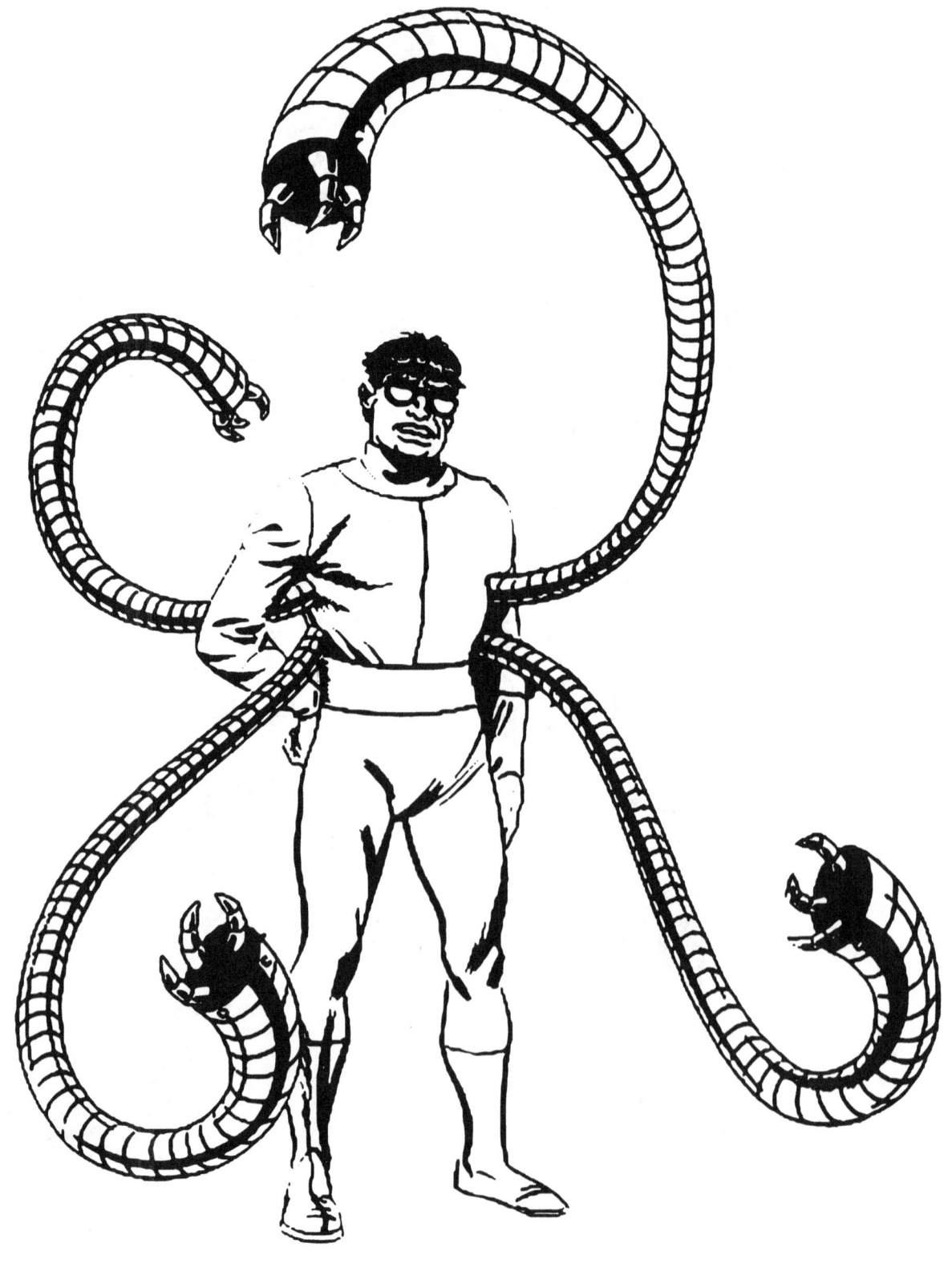

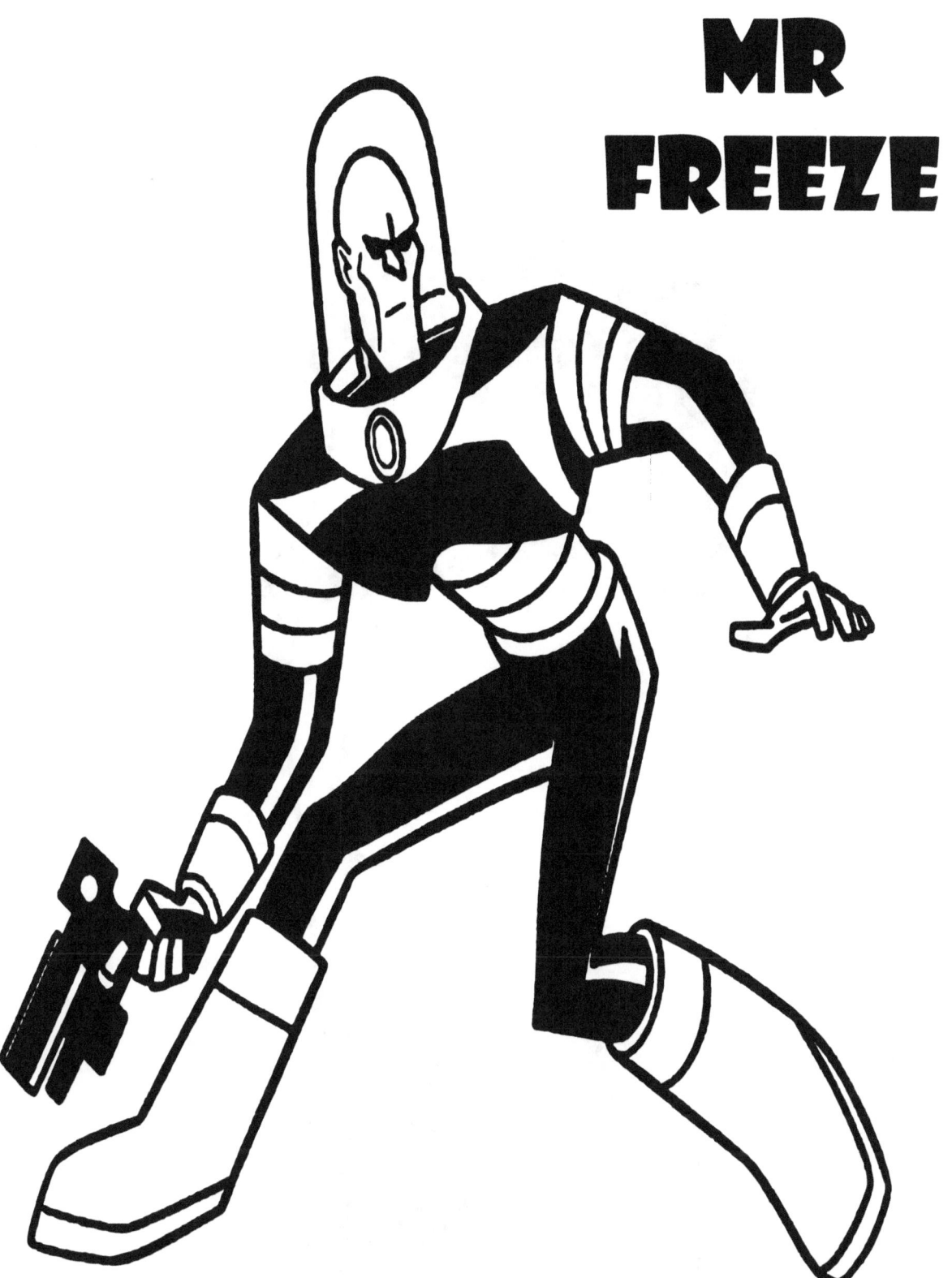

MR
FREEZE

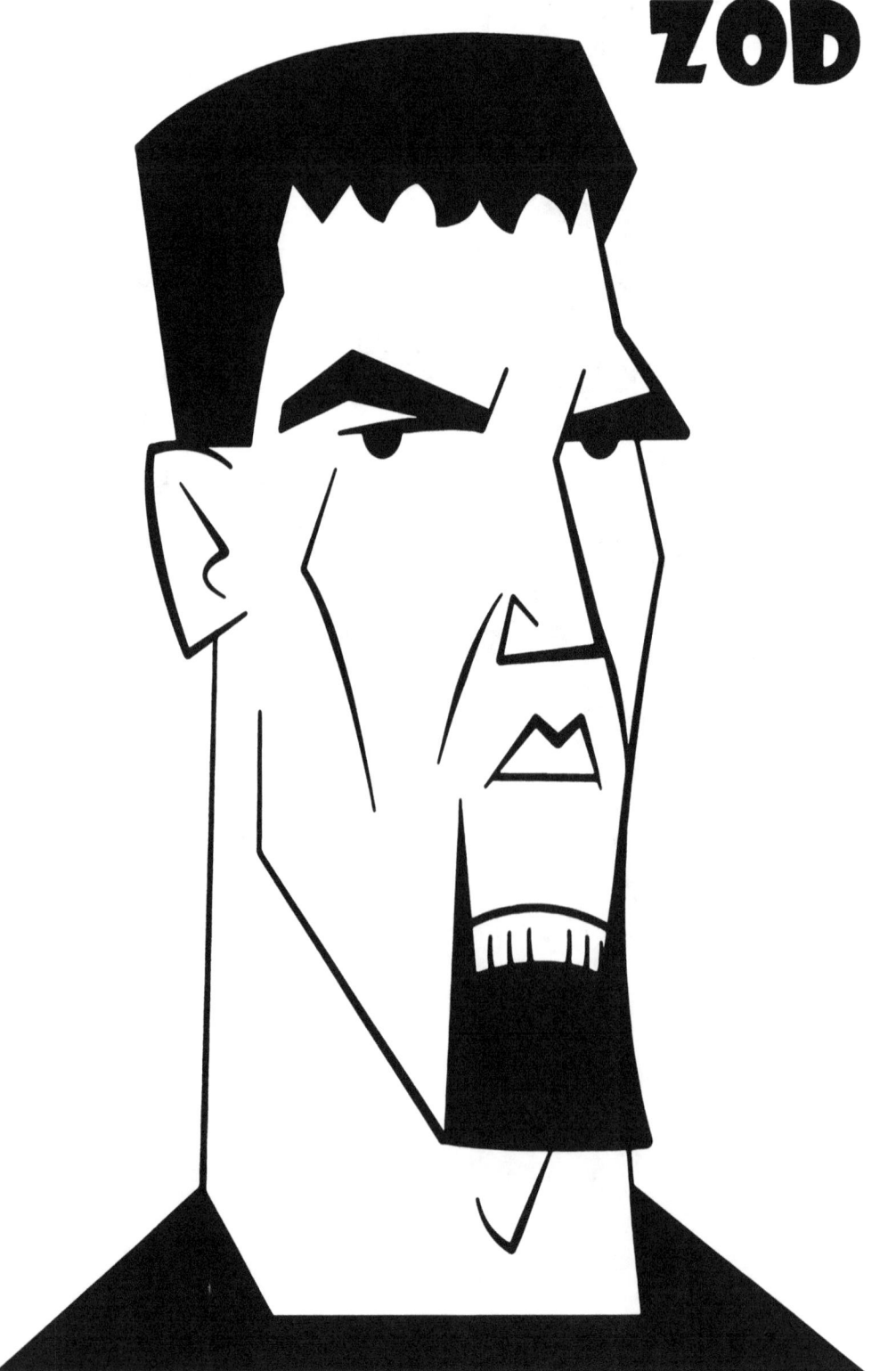

DEADPOOL

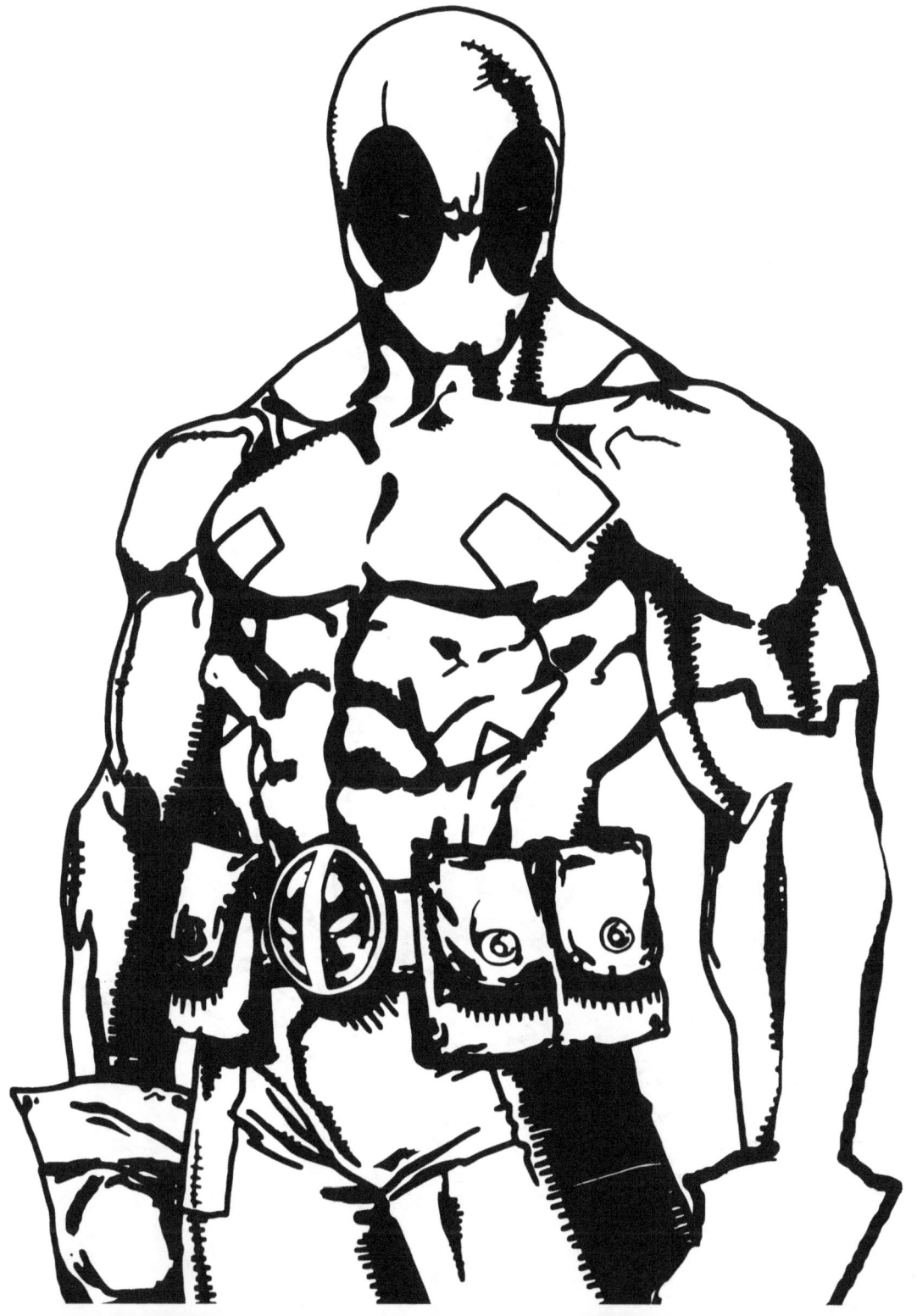

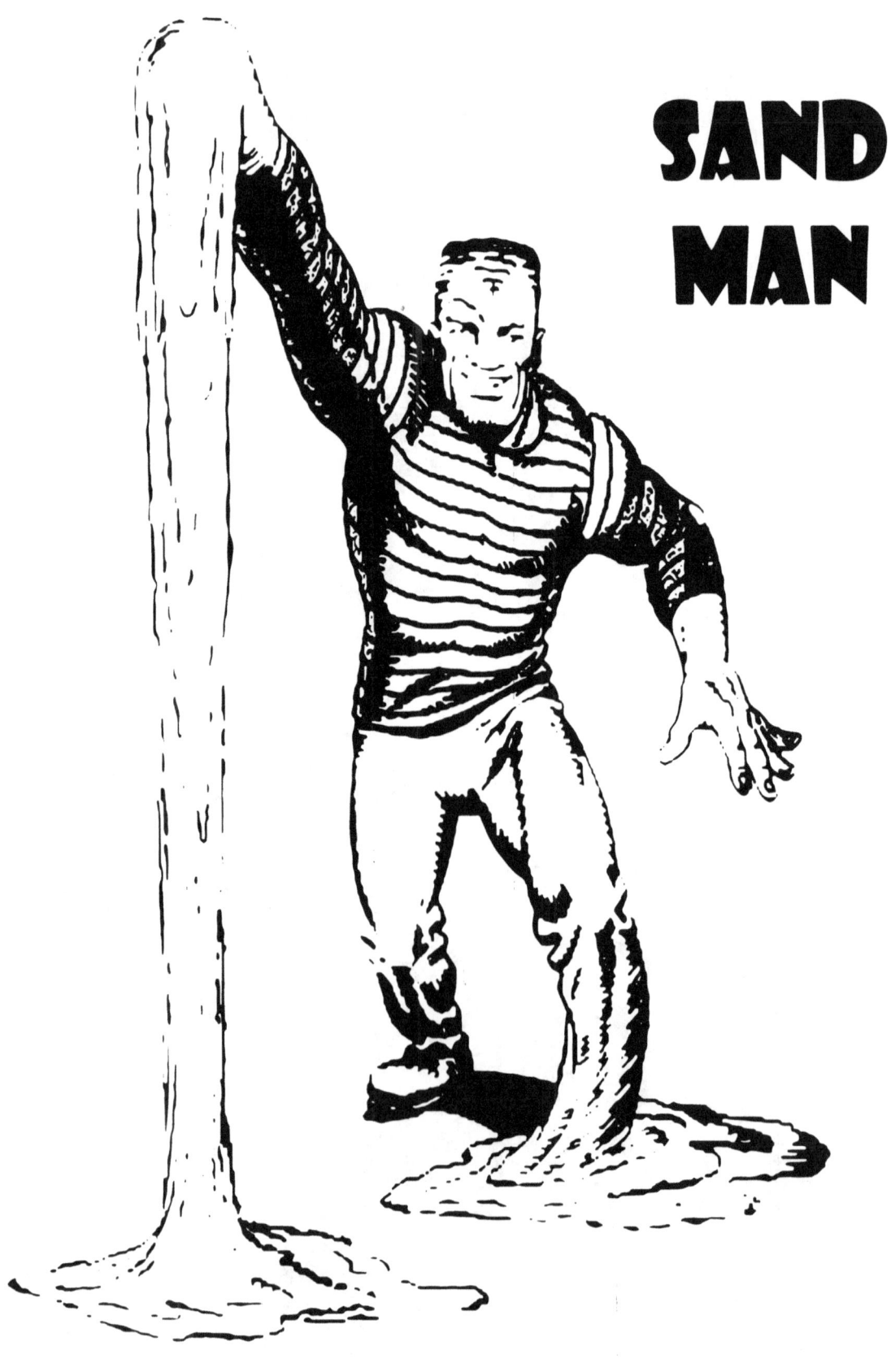

SAND MAN

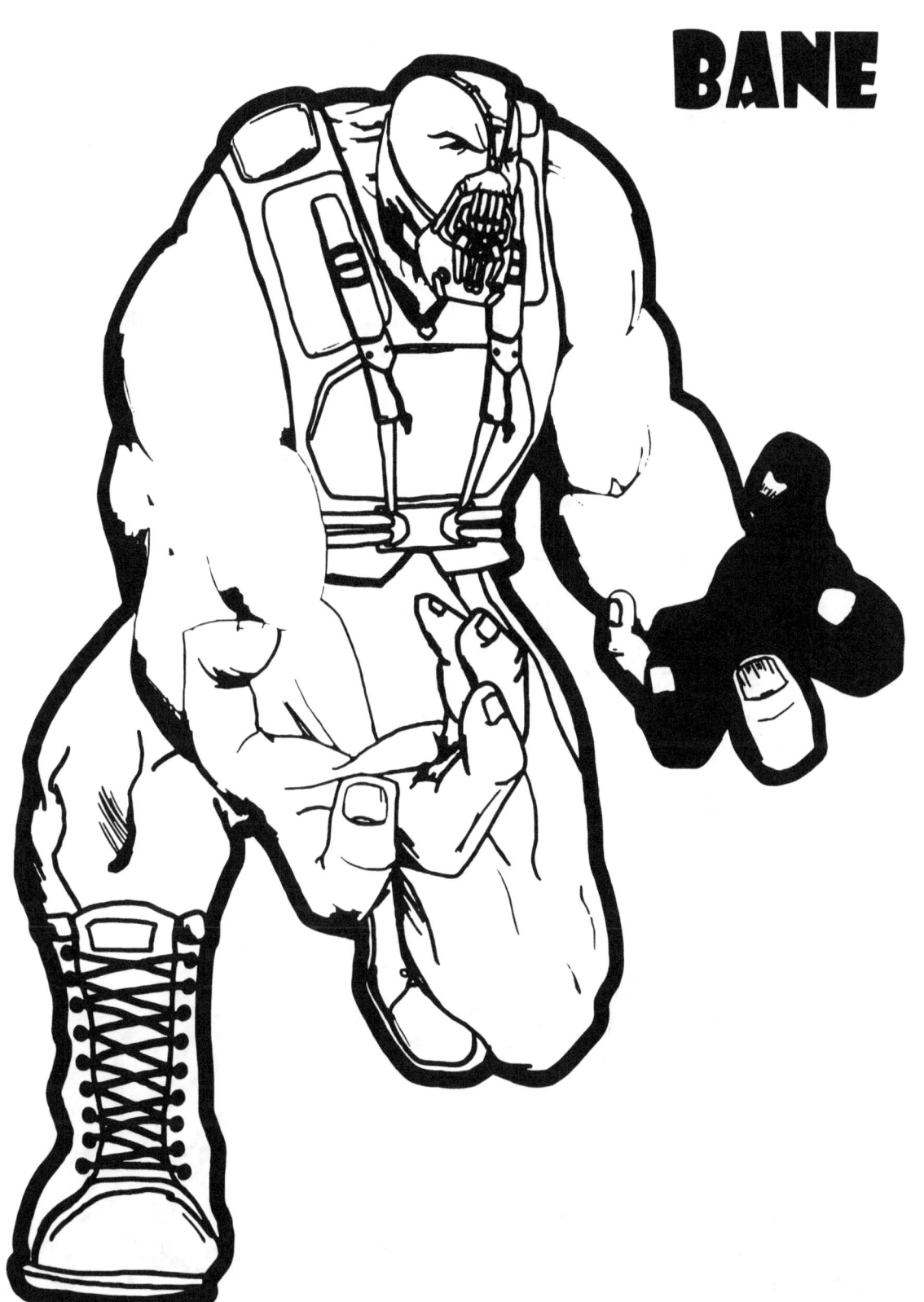

BANE

SHREDDER

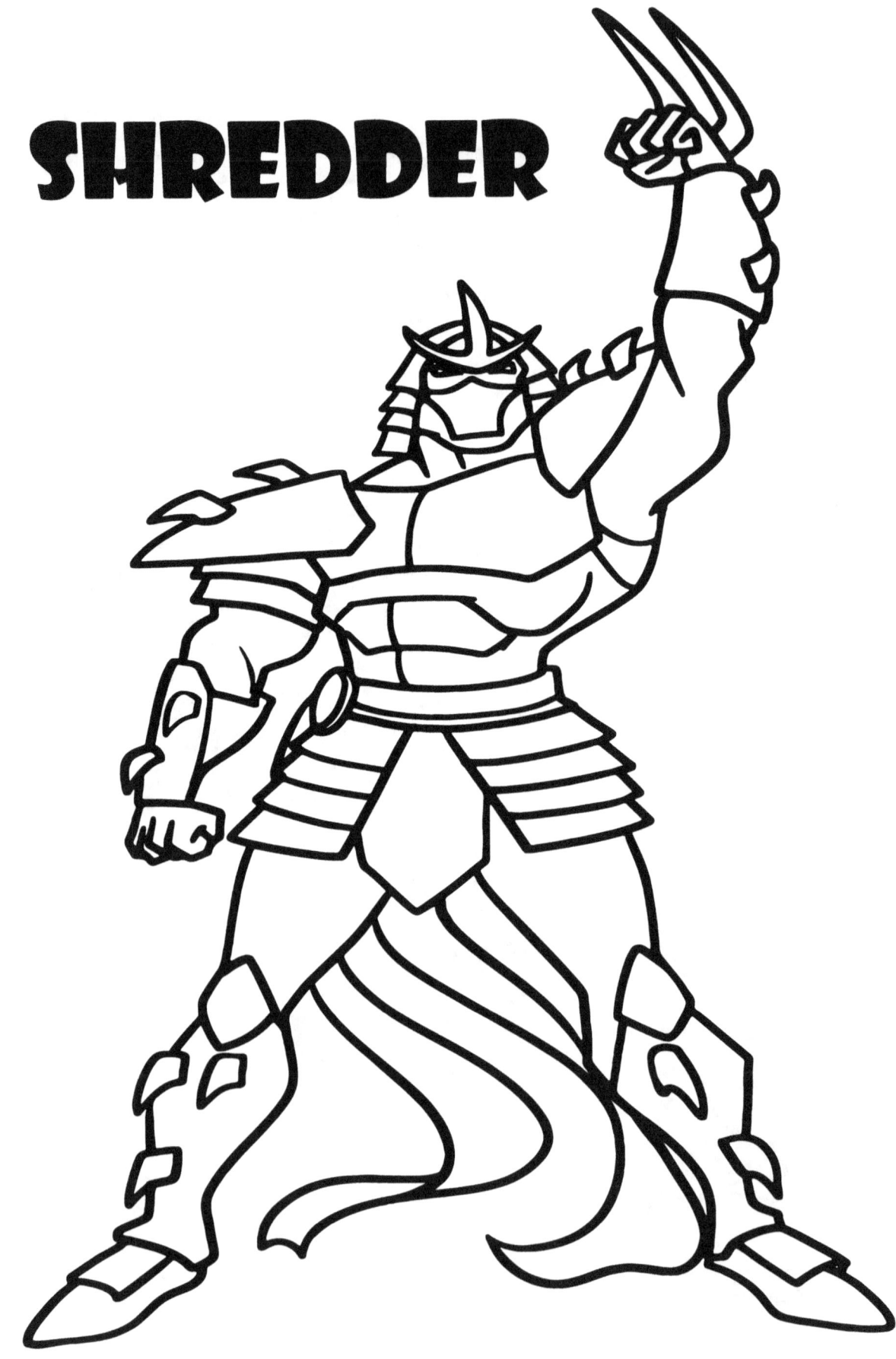

HARLEY QUINN

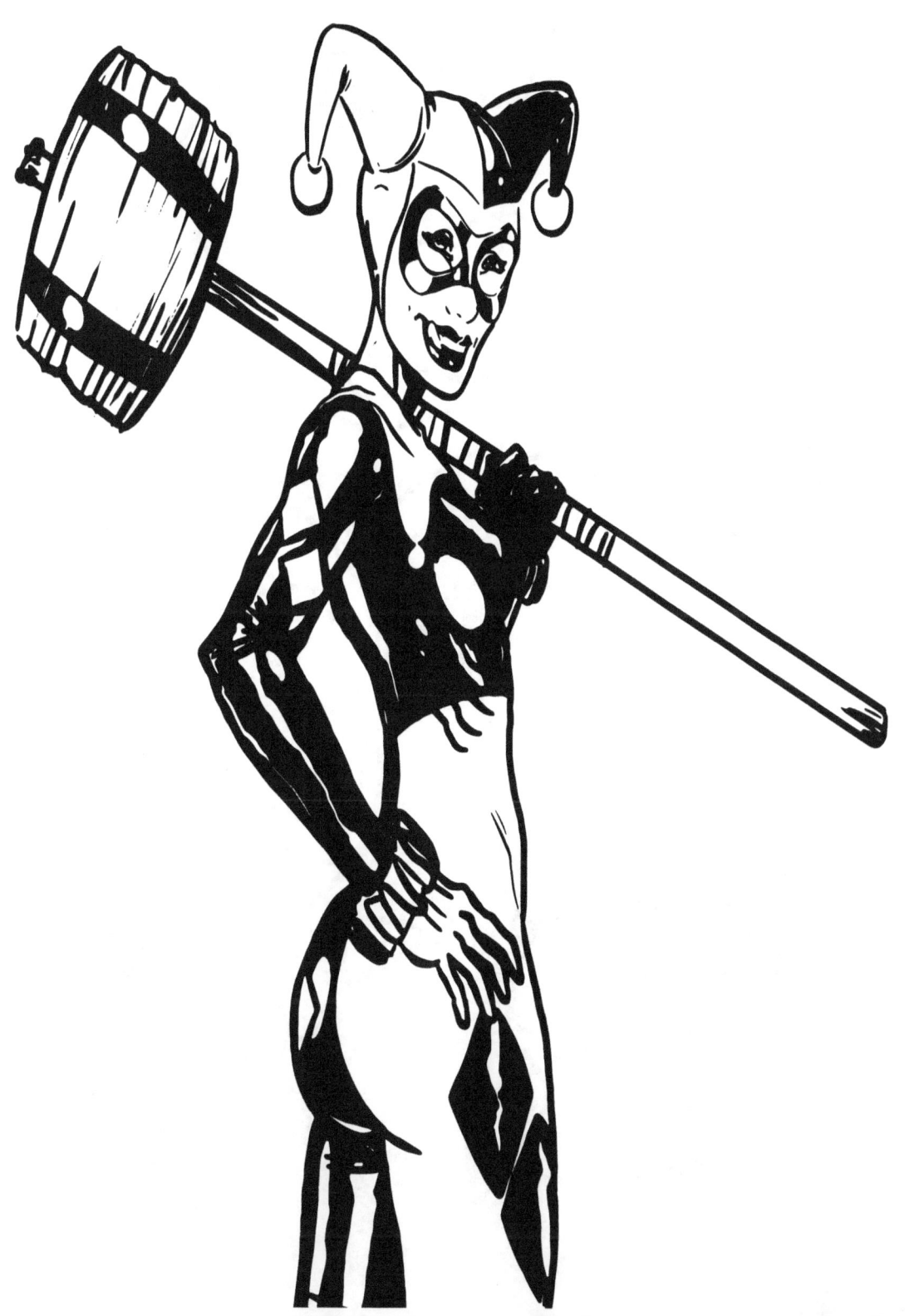

ABOMINATION

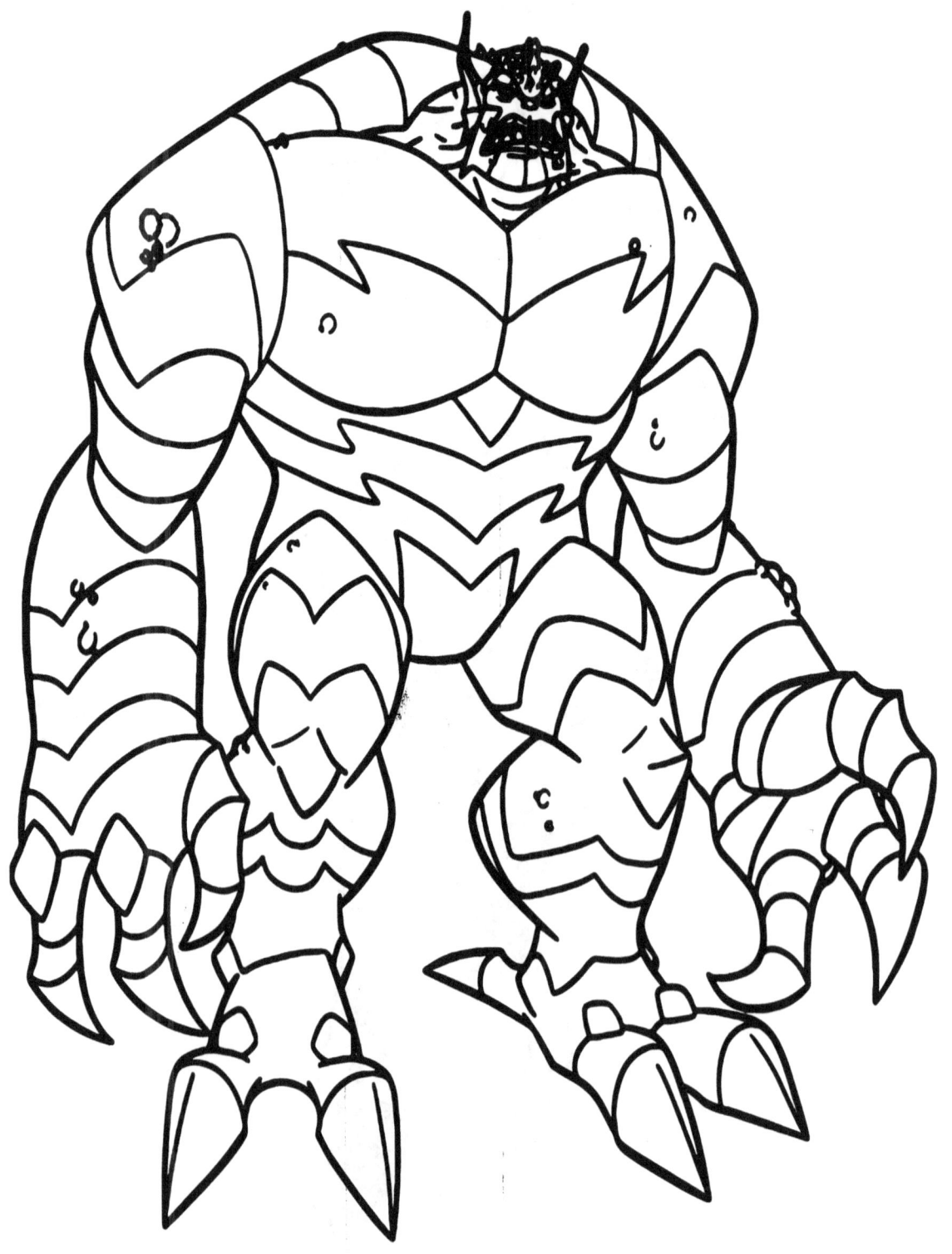

LIZARD

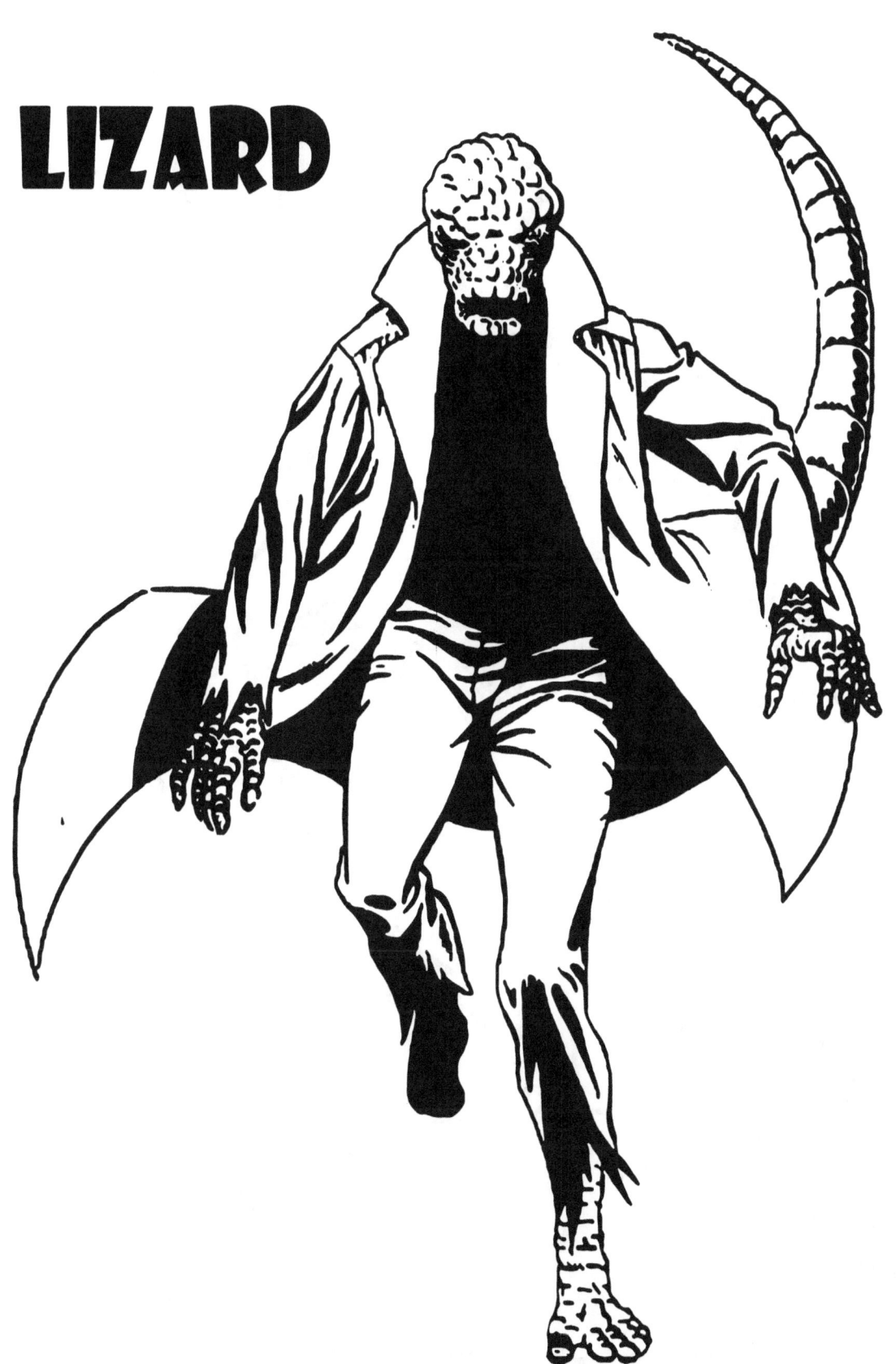

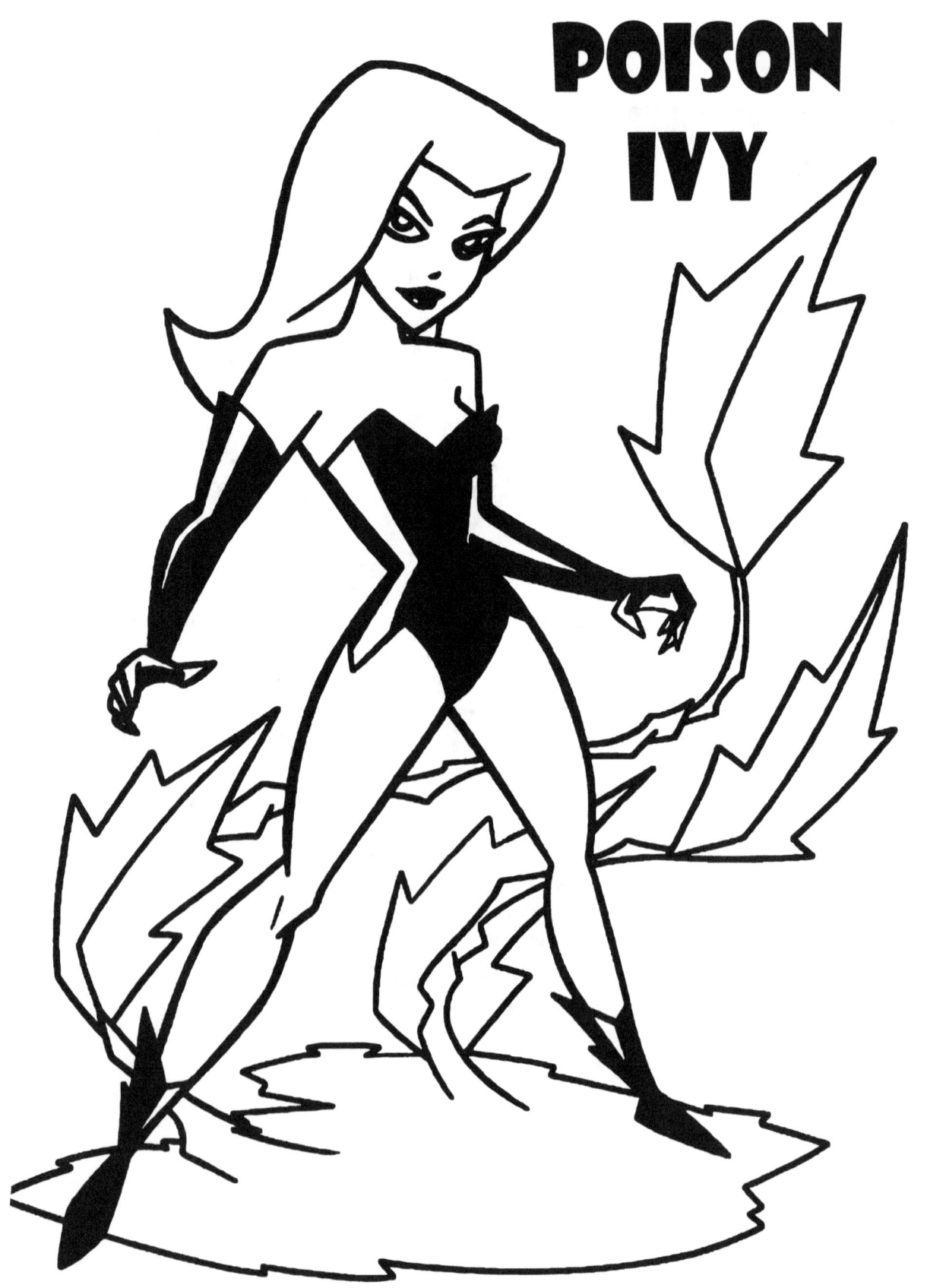

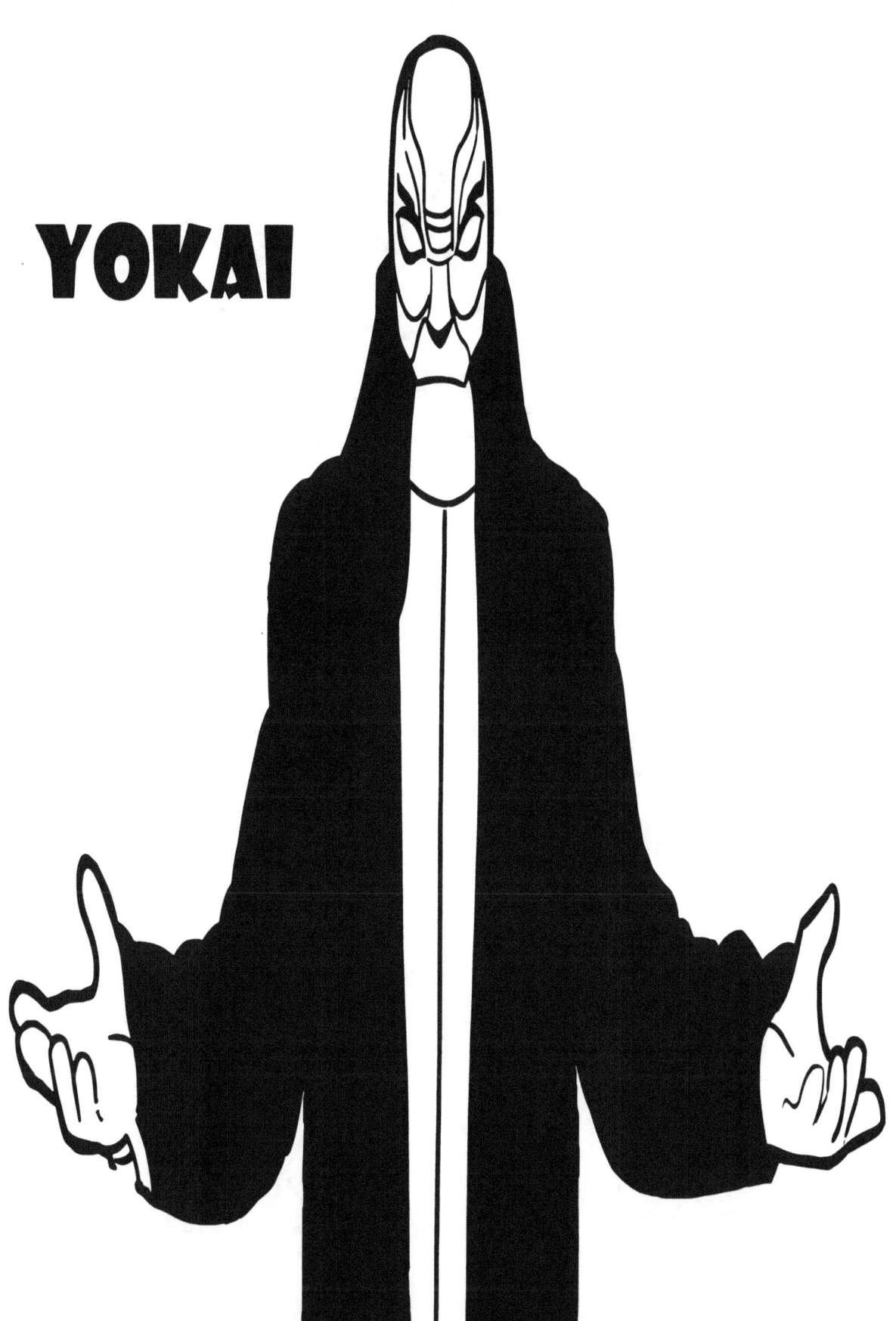

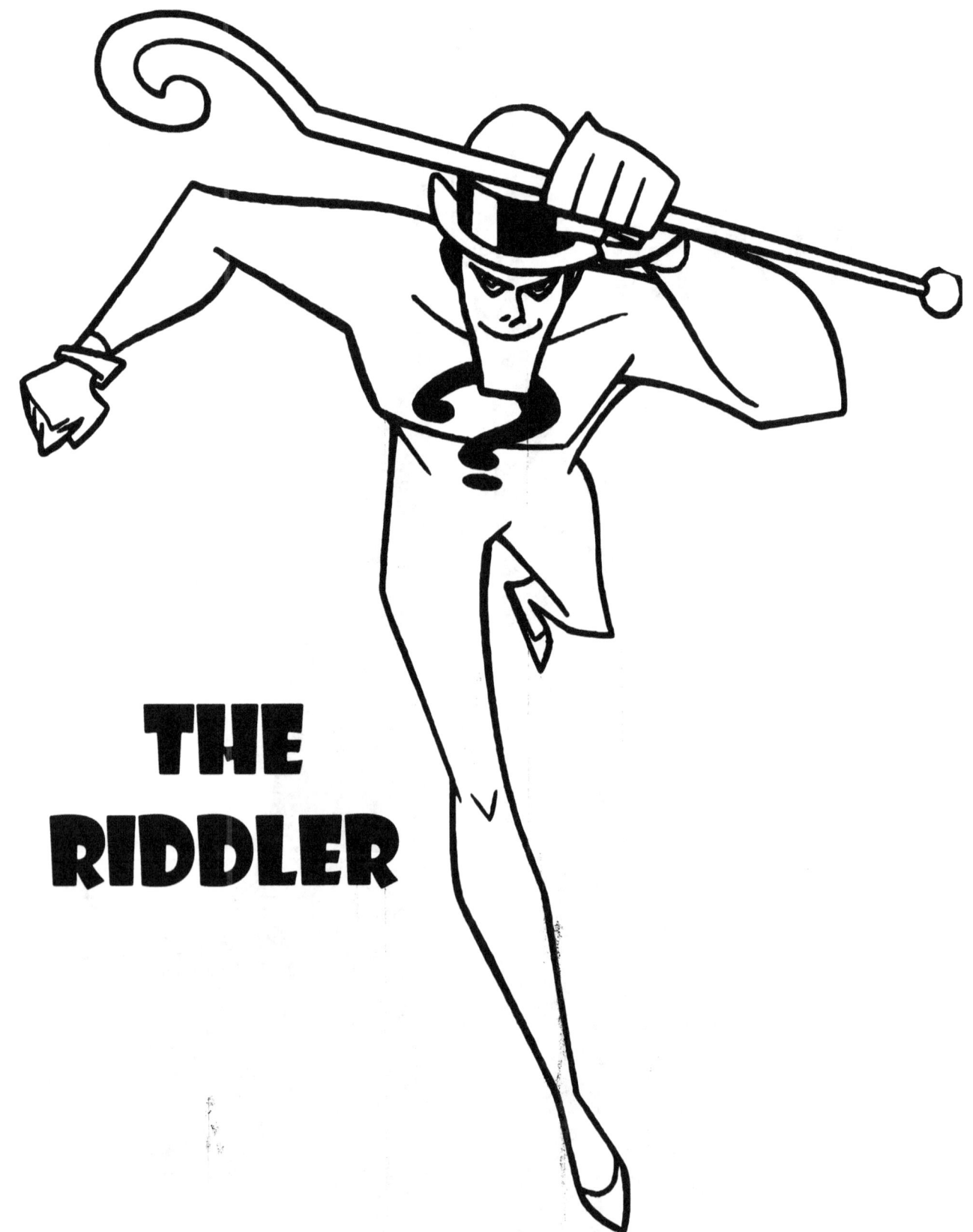

THE
RIDDLER

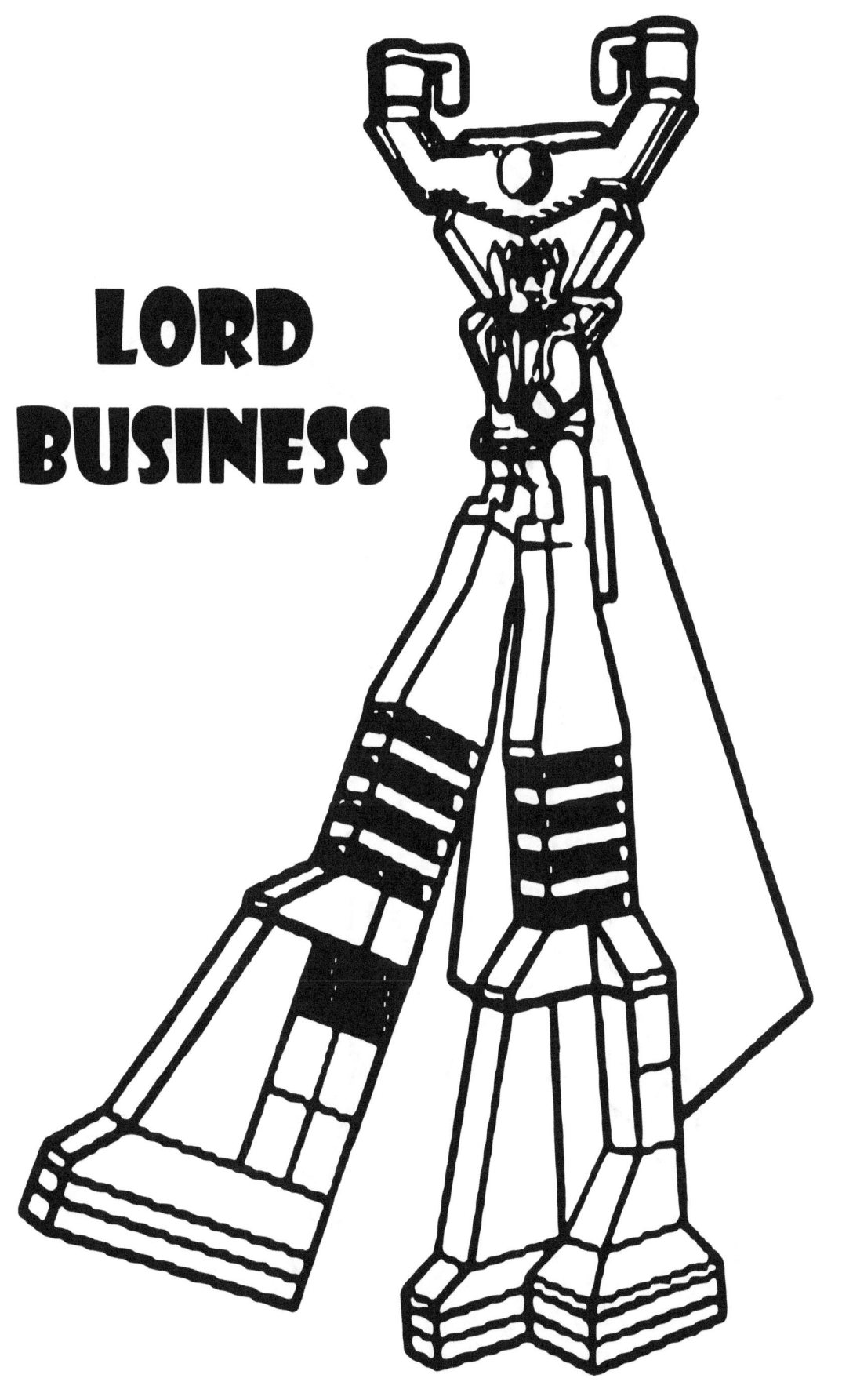

LORD
BUSINESS

SYNDROME

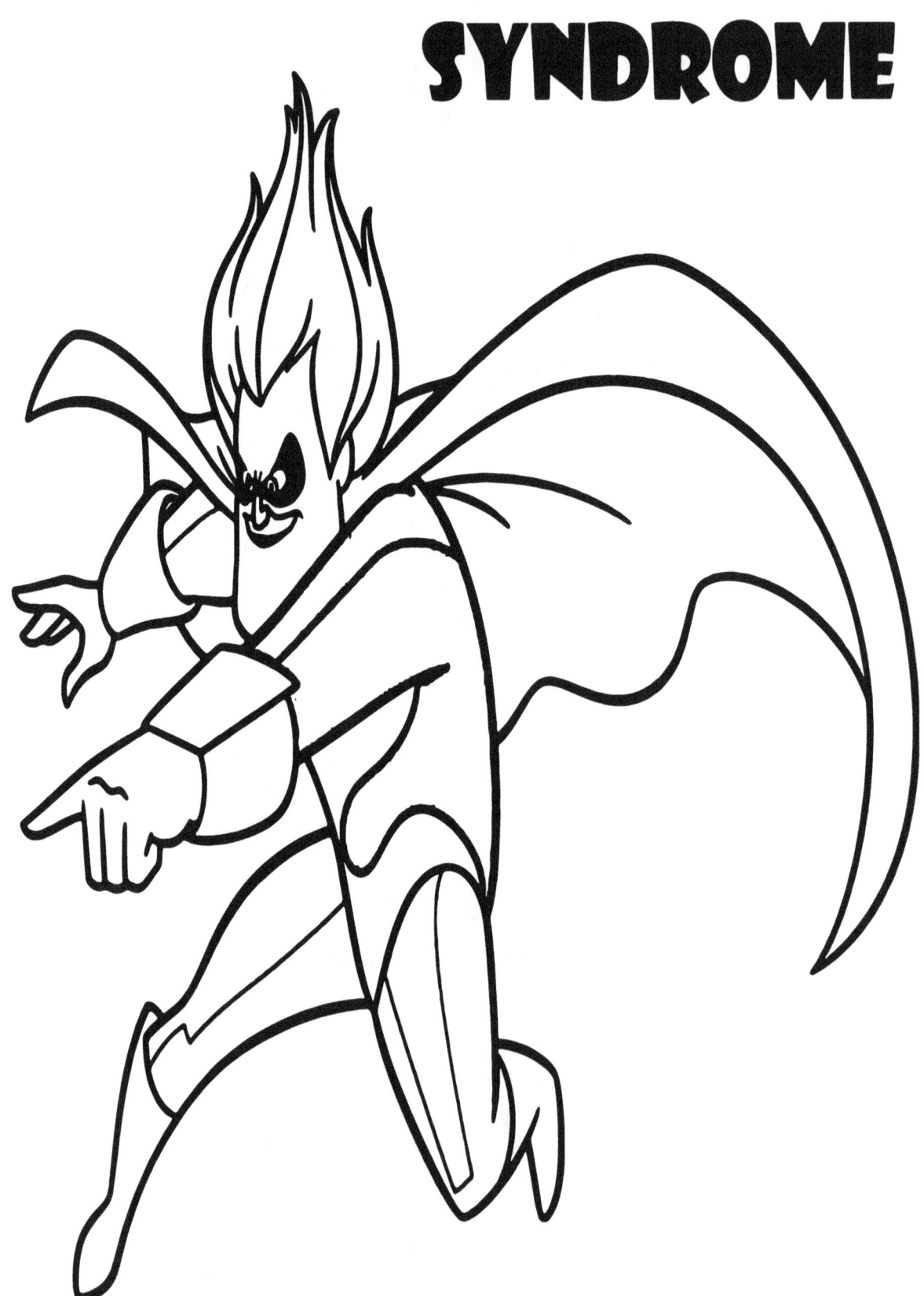

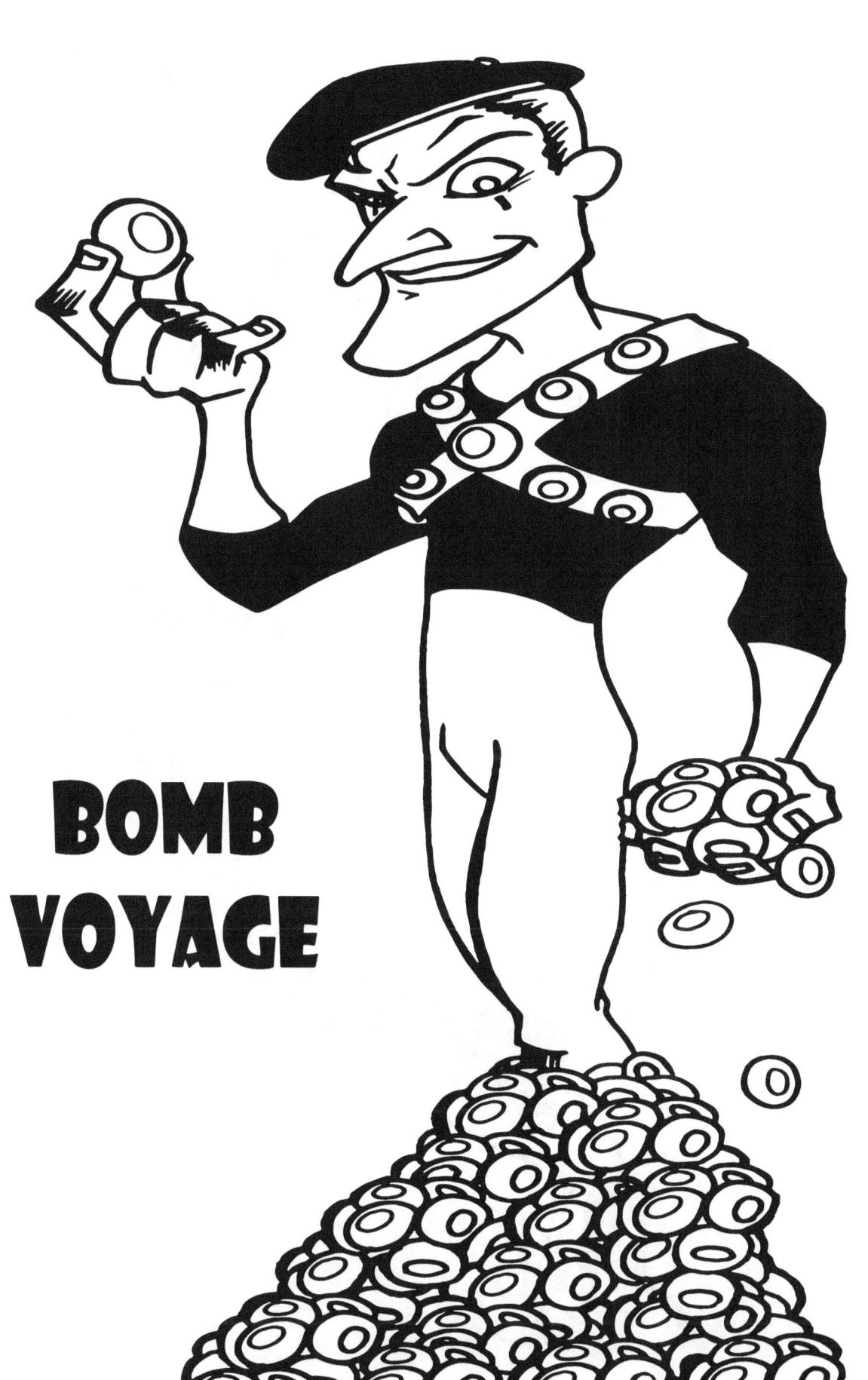

BOMB
VOYAGE

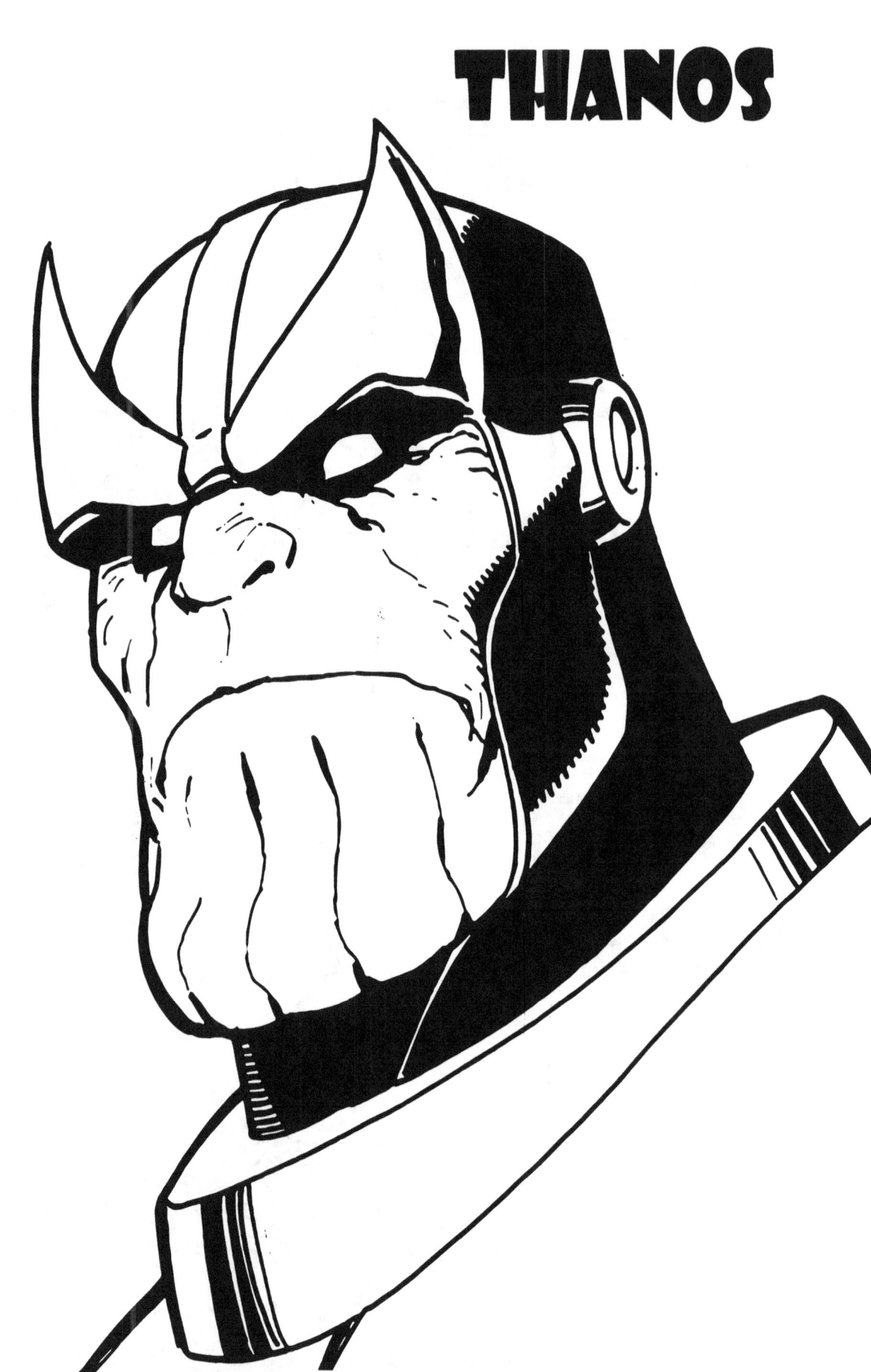

THANOS

SABRETOOTH

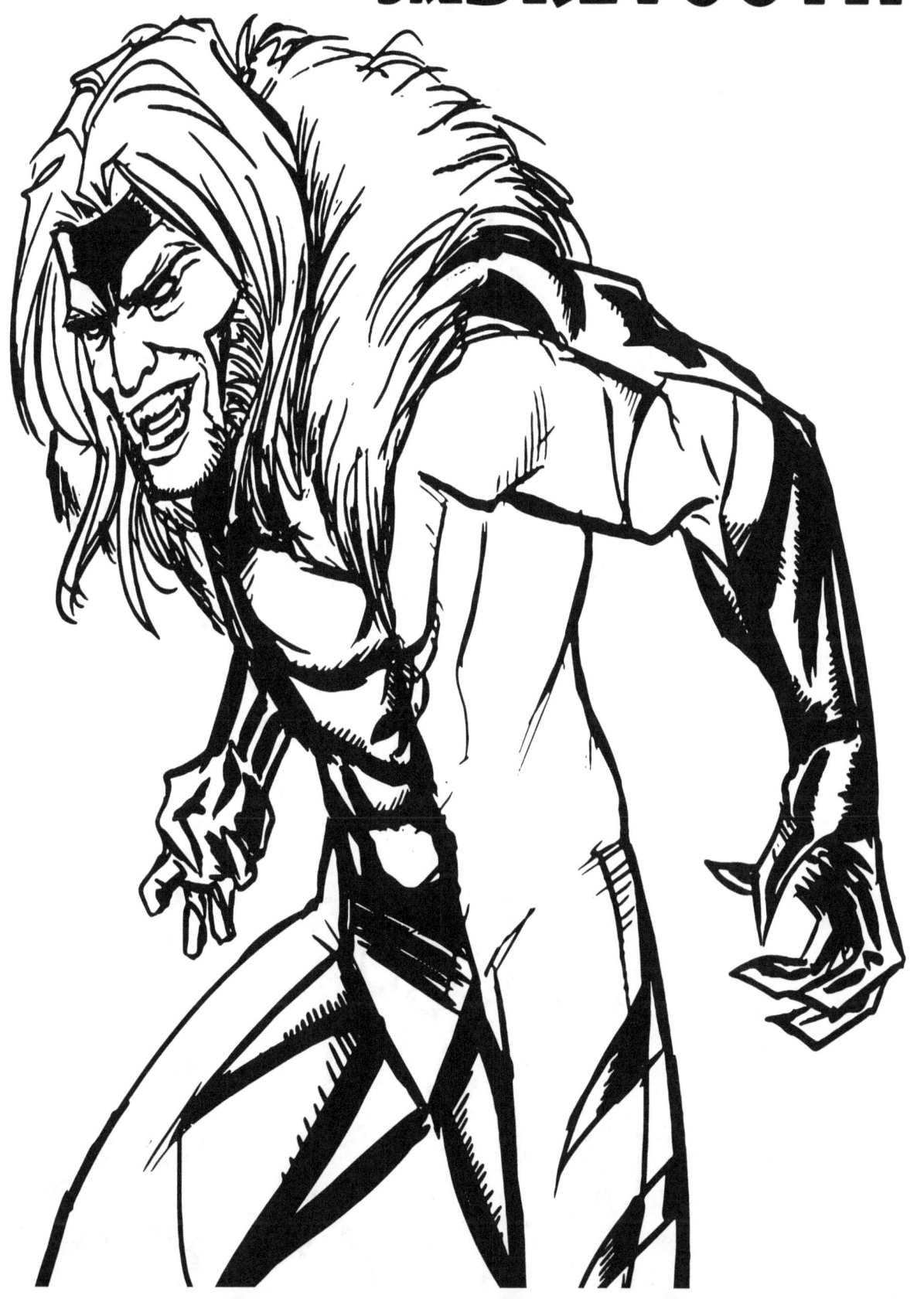

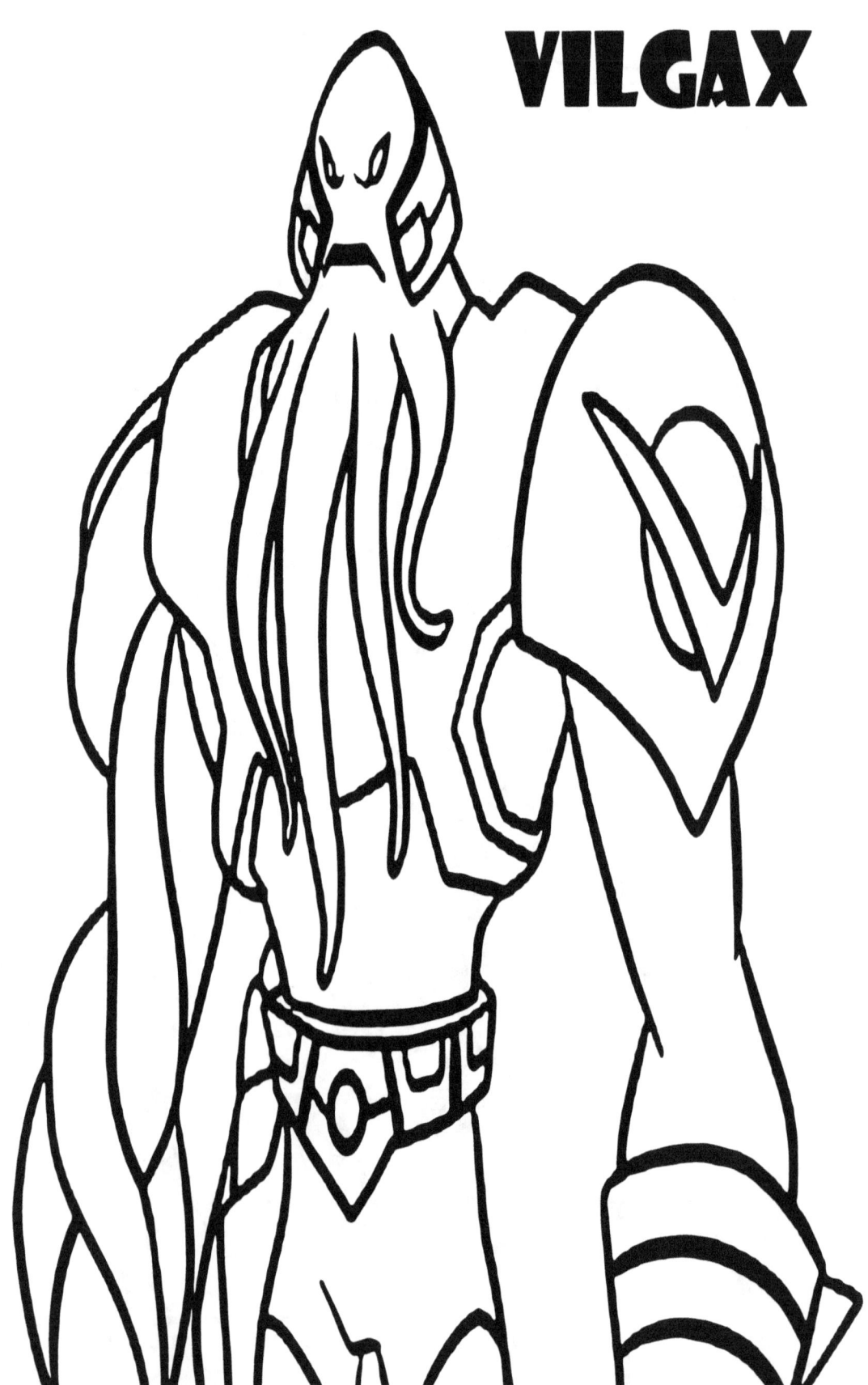

VILGAX

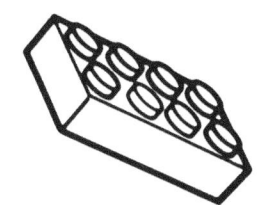

LEGO

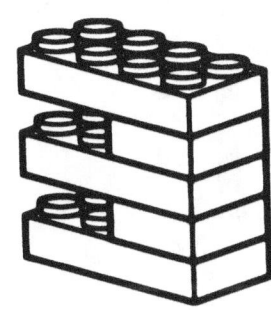

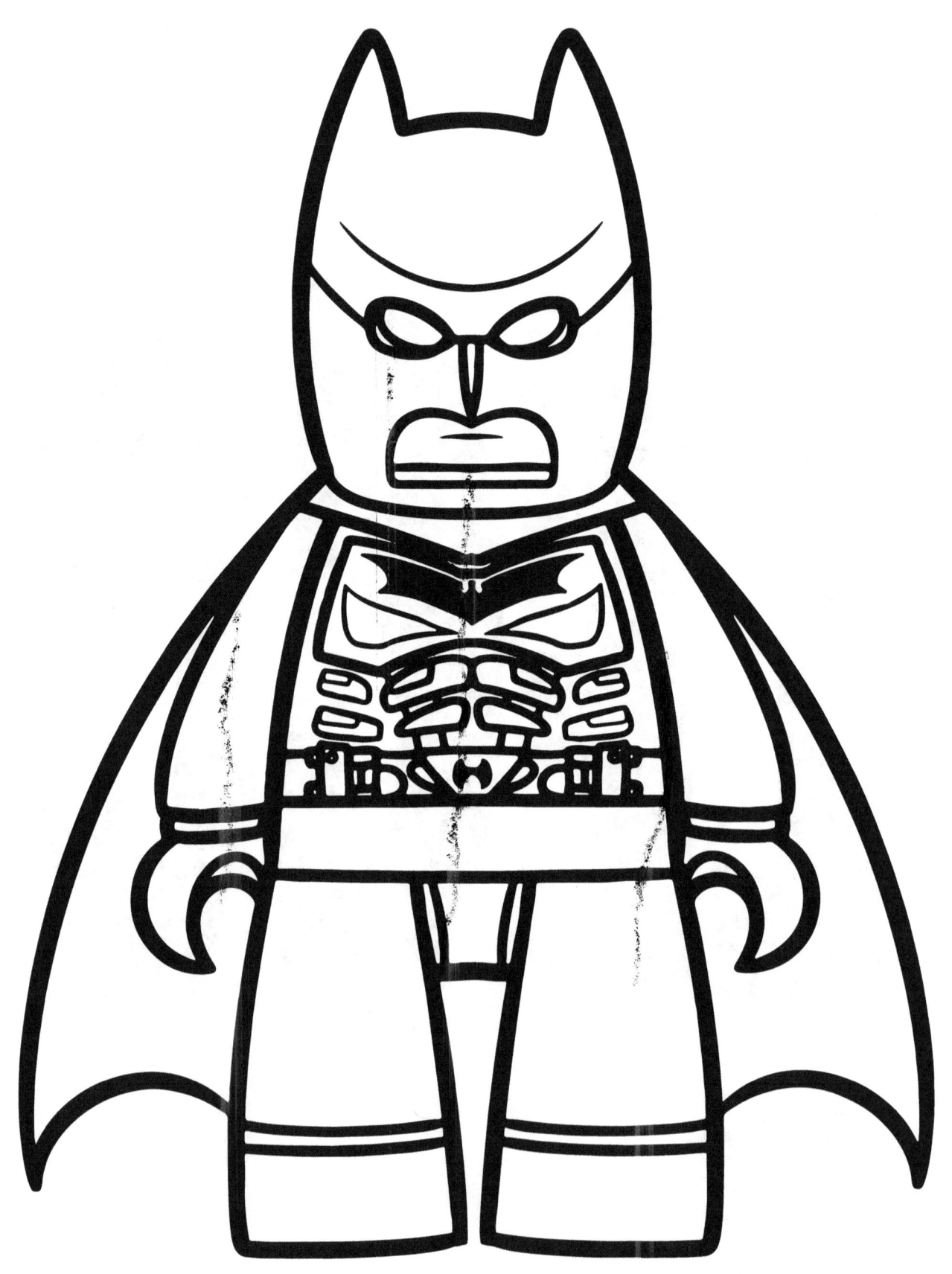

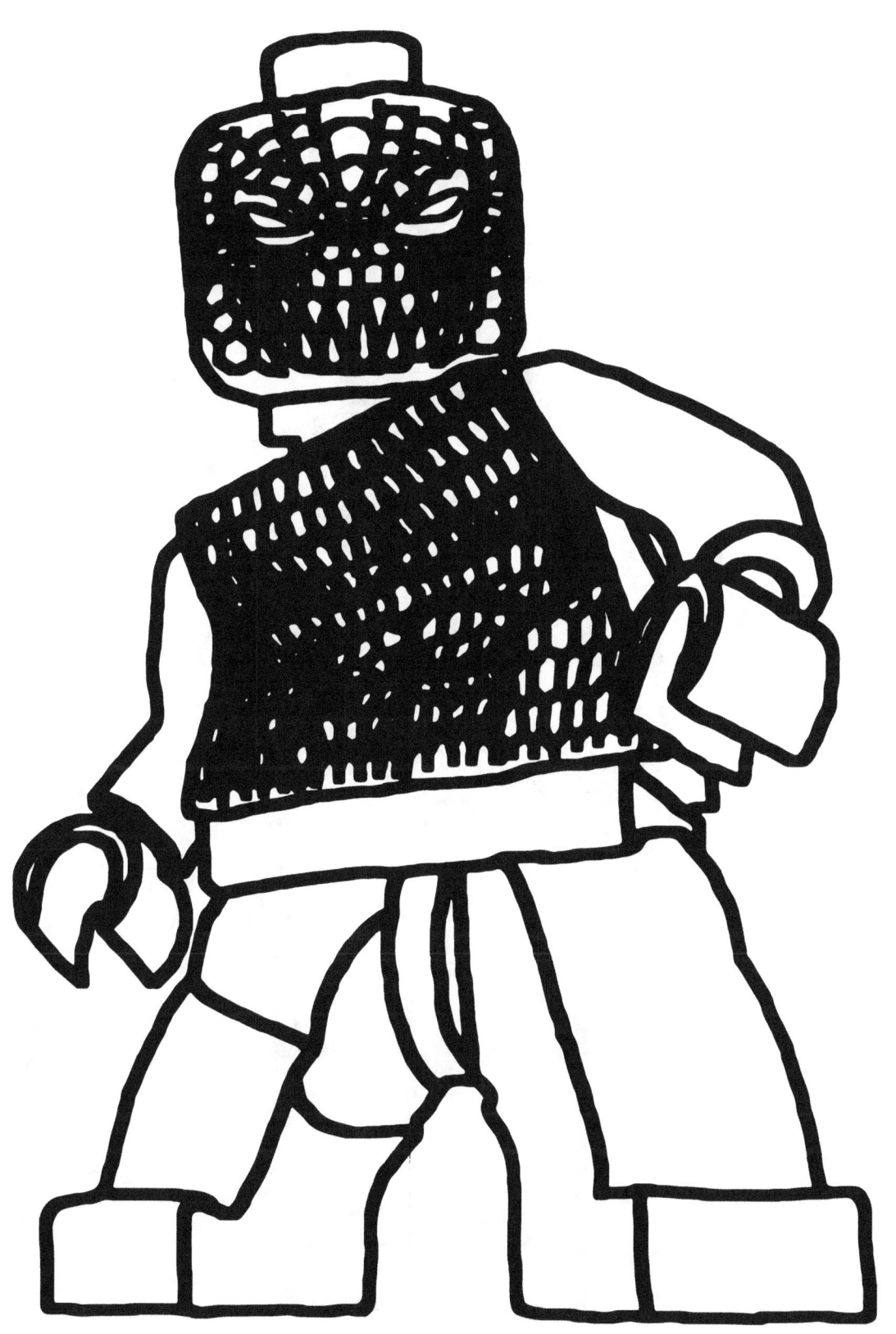

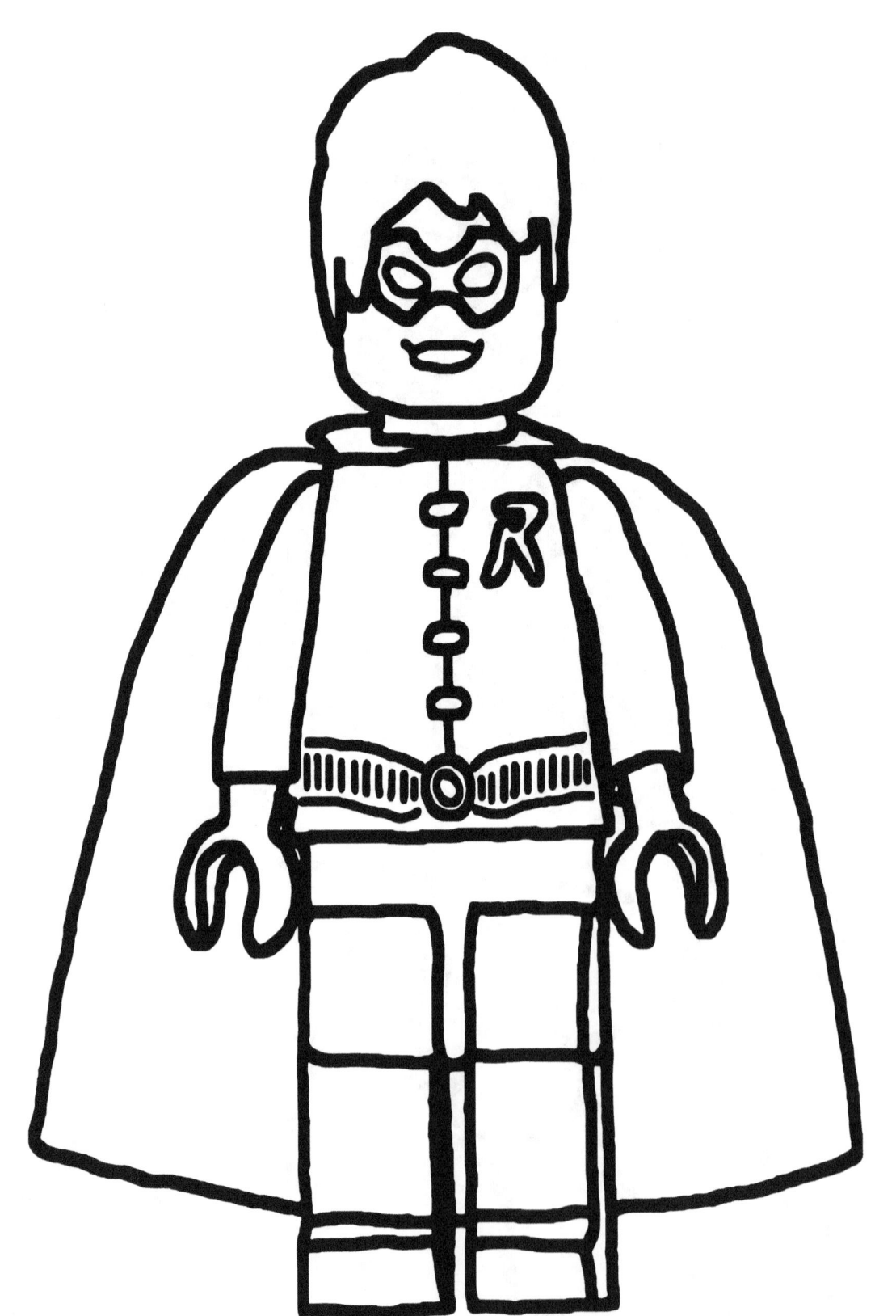

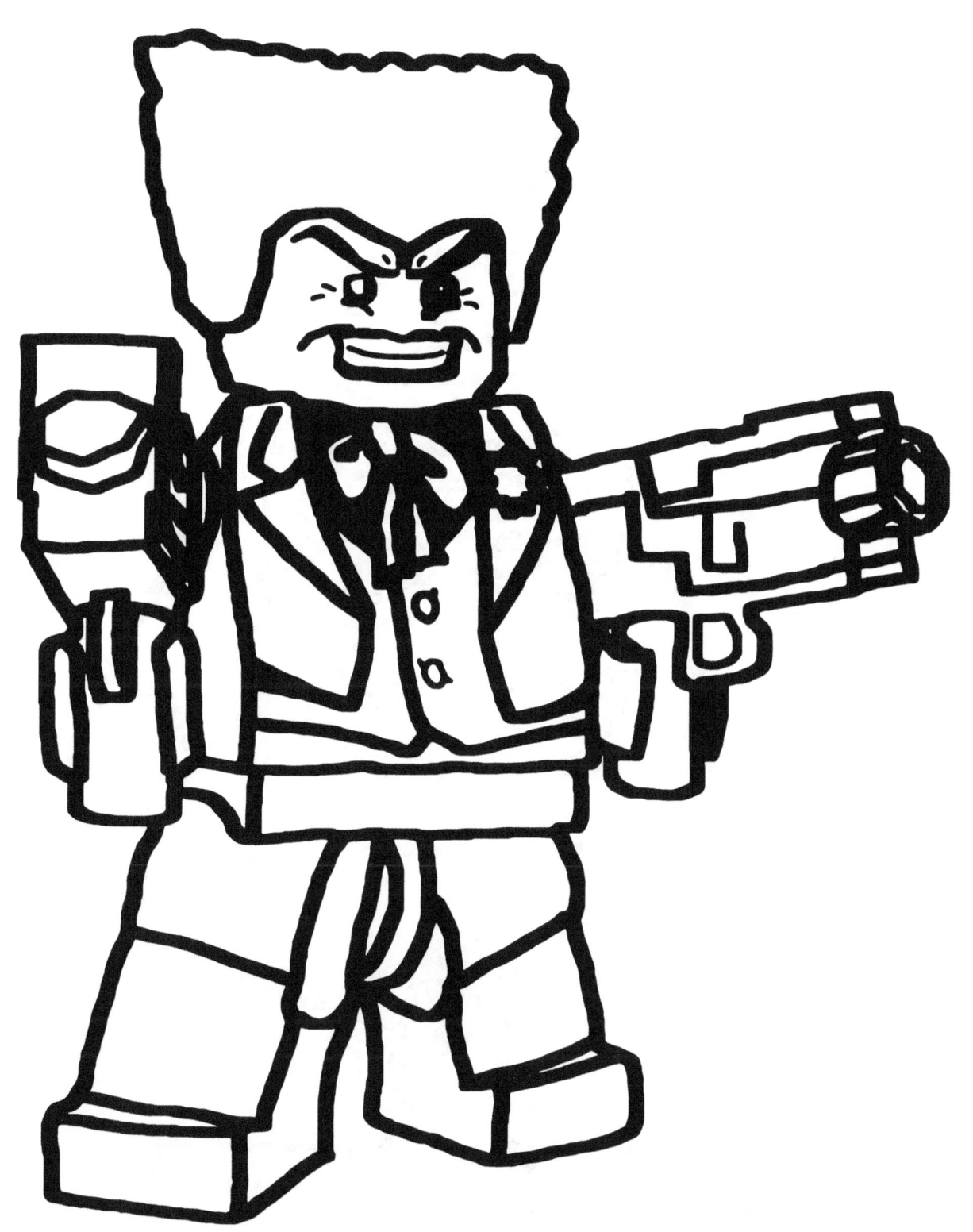

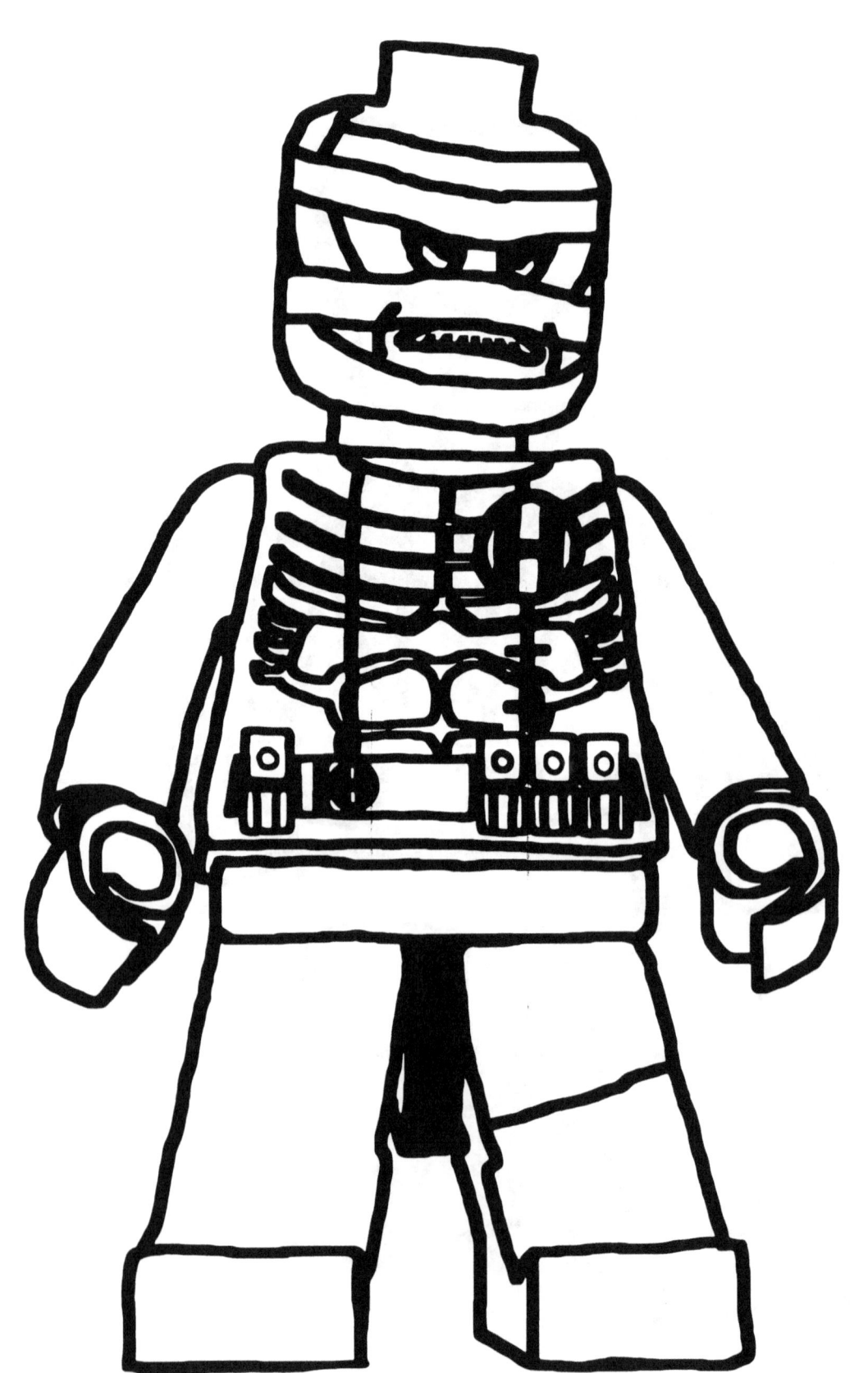

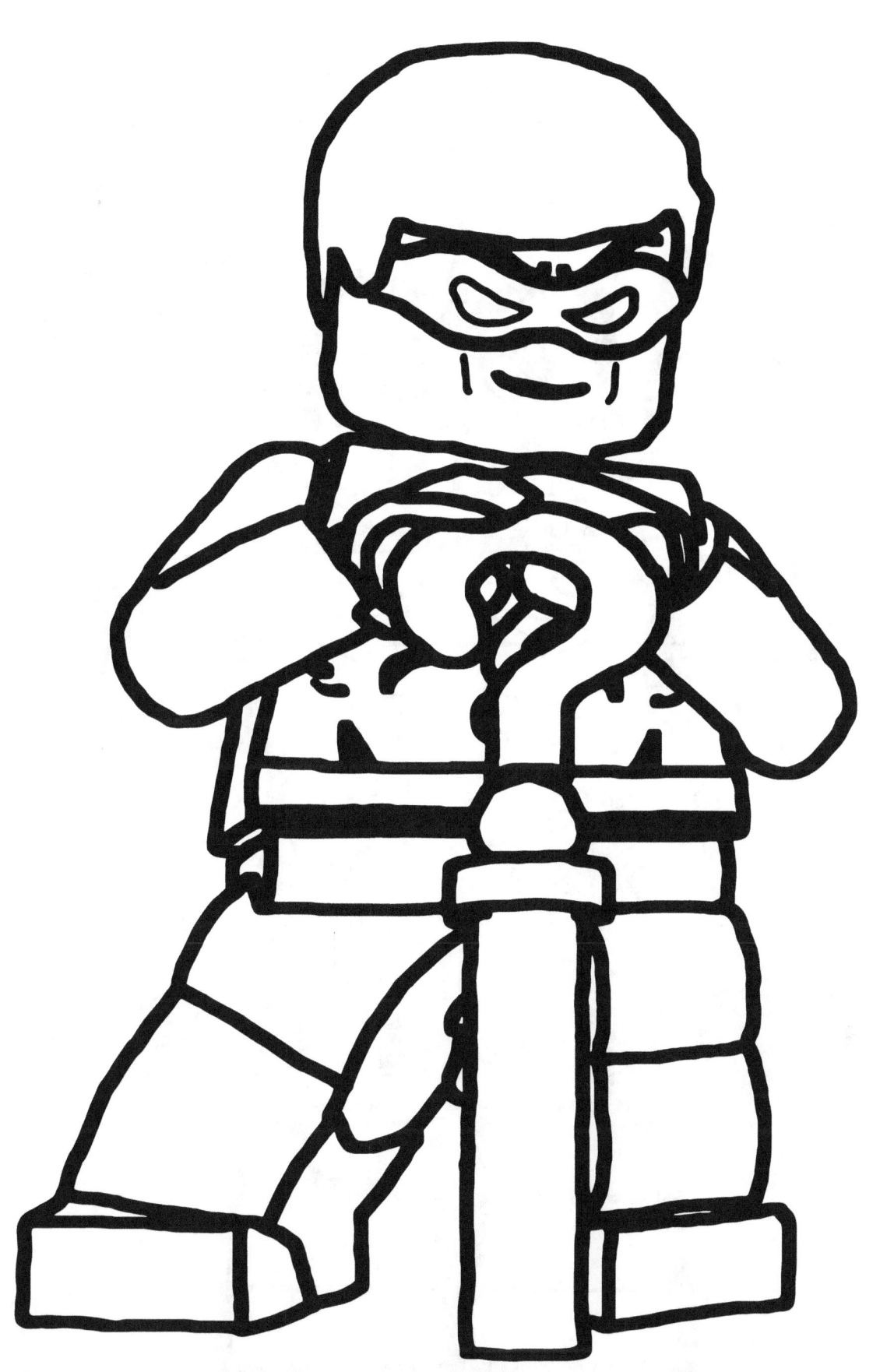

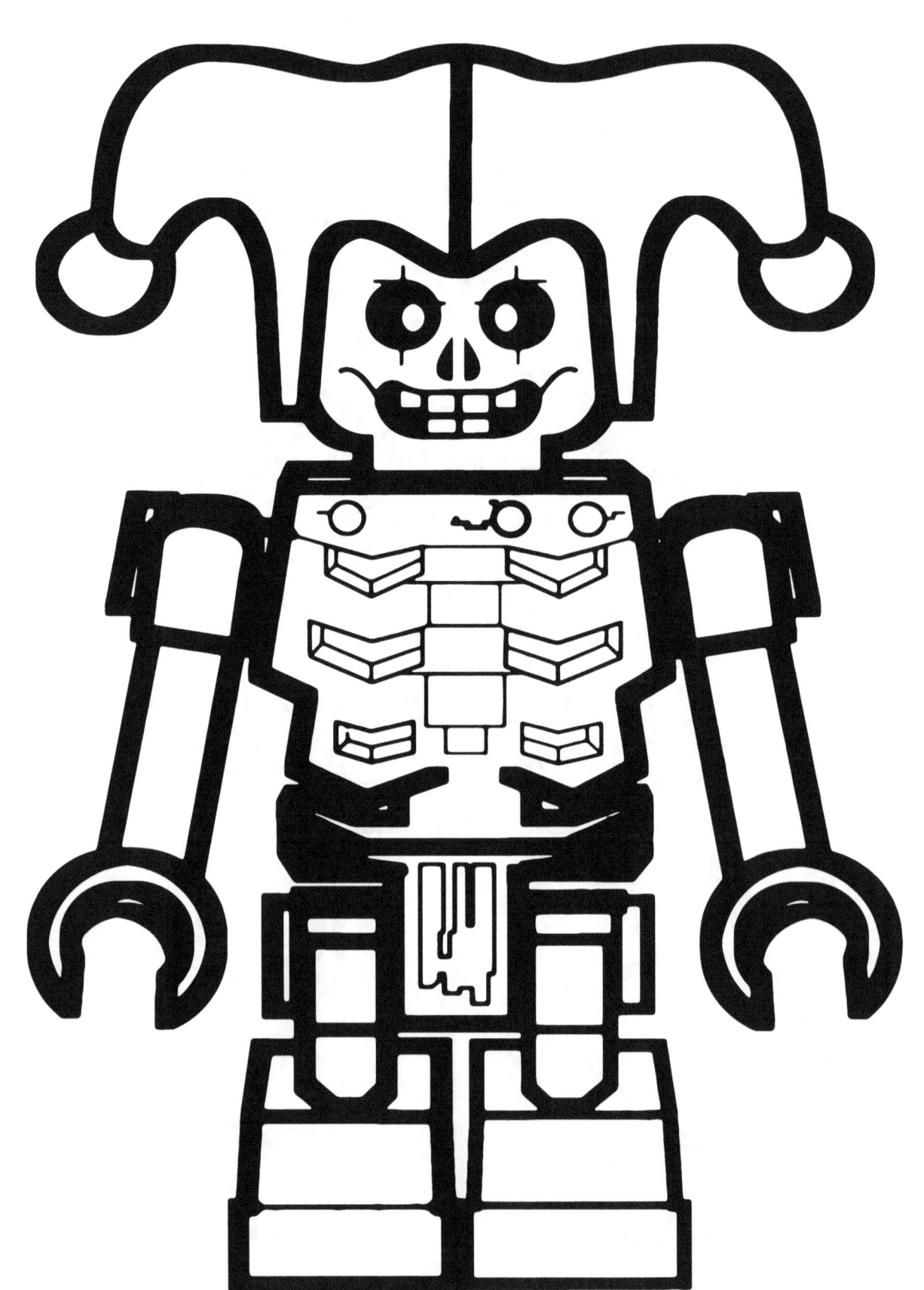

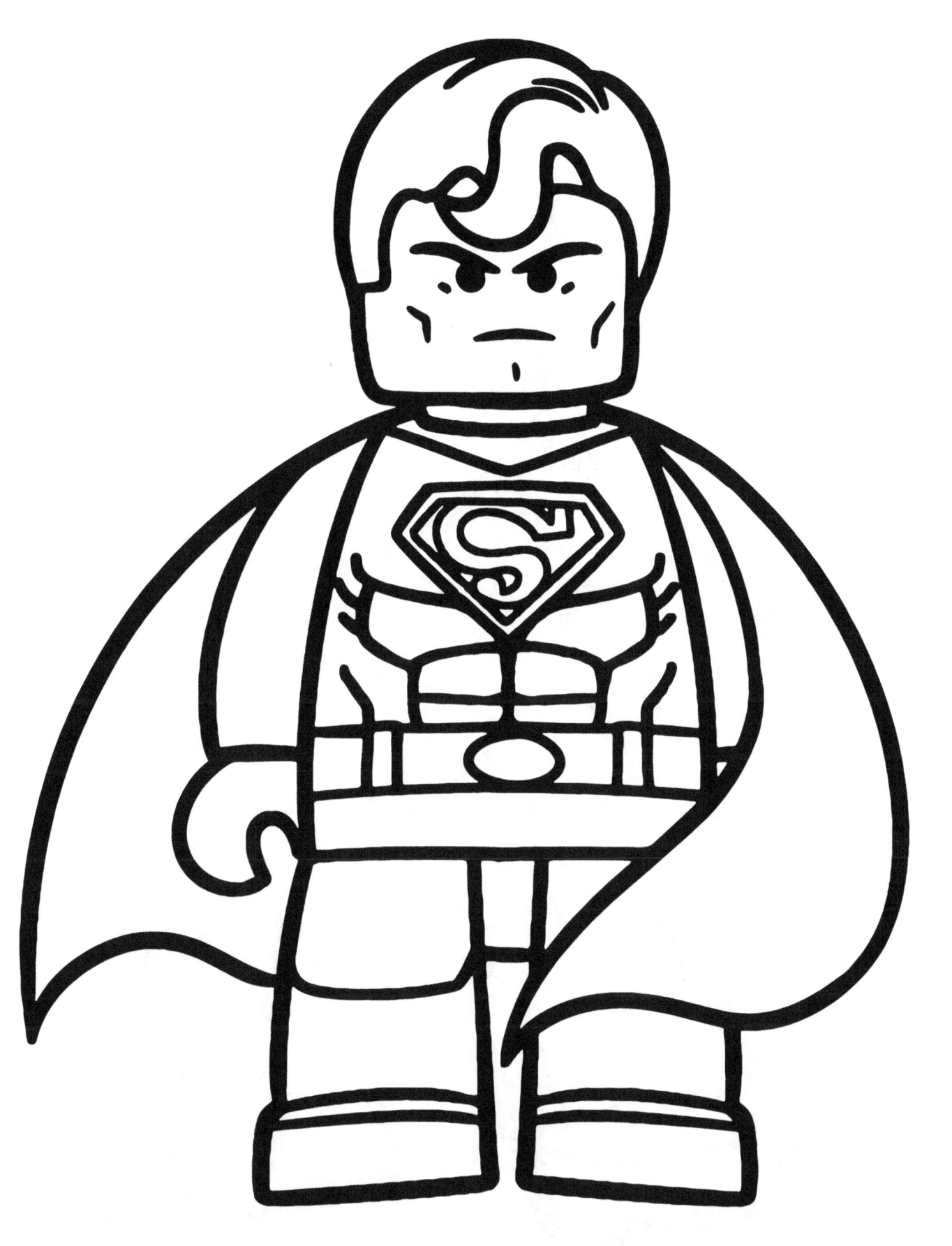

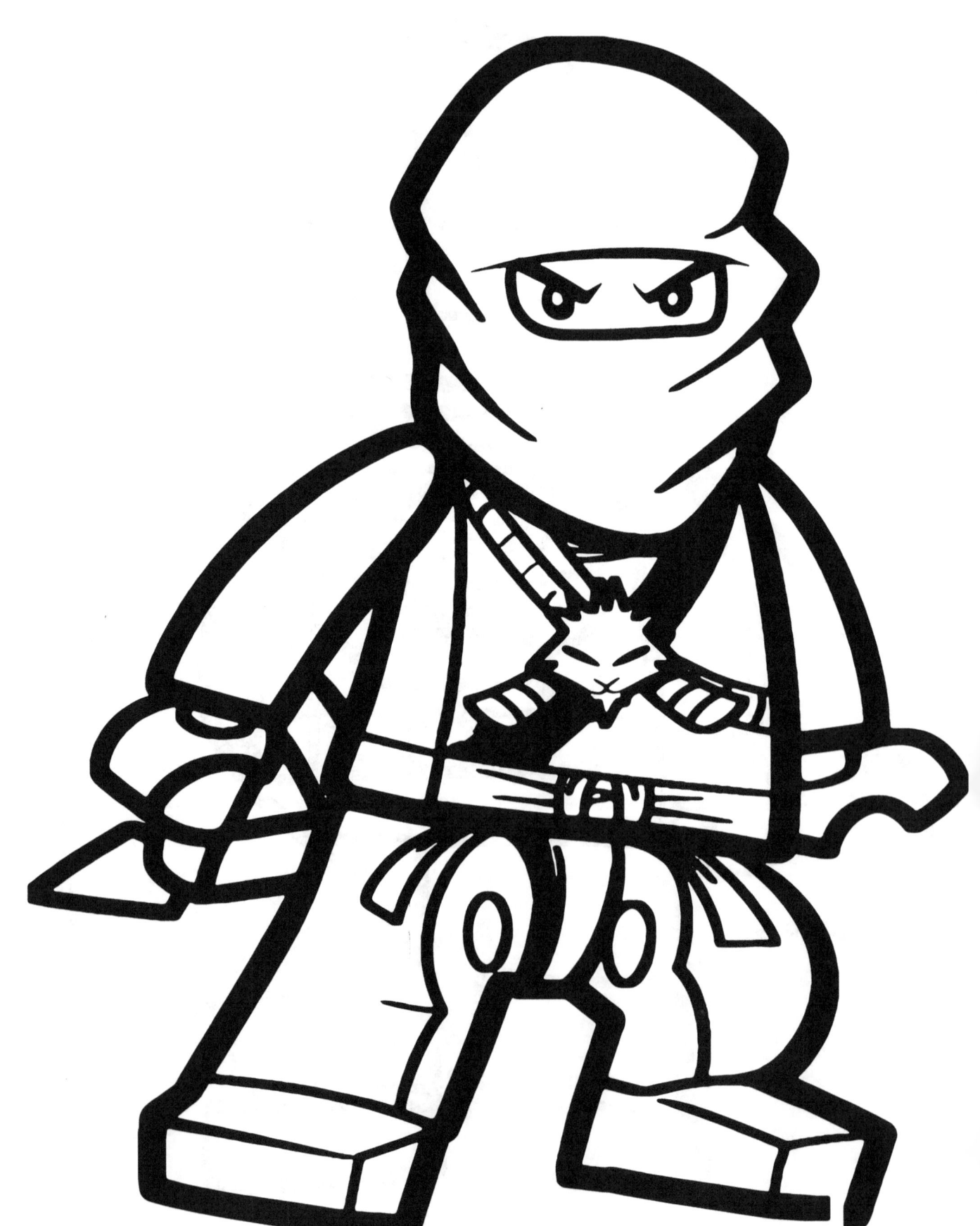

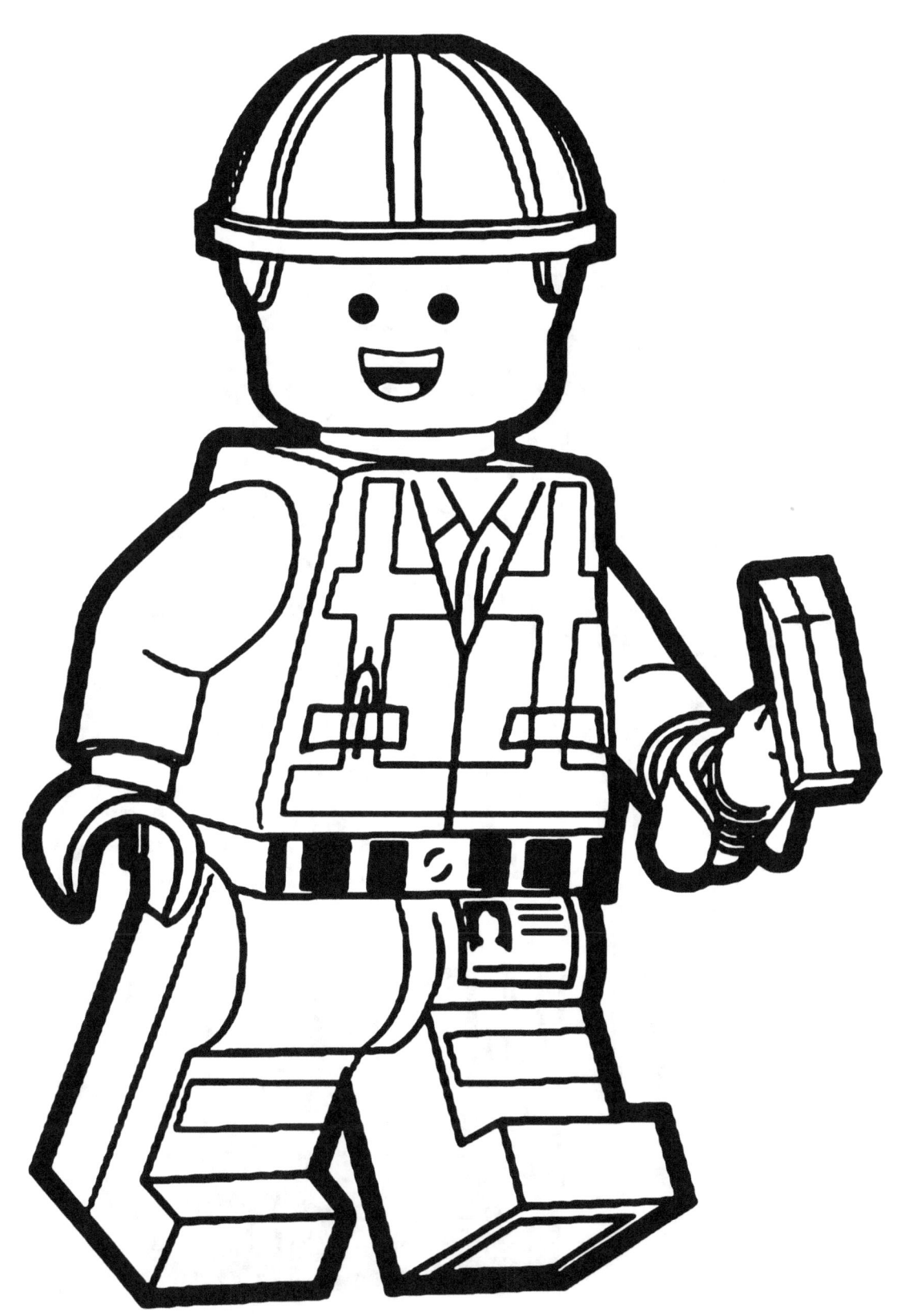

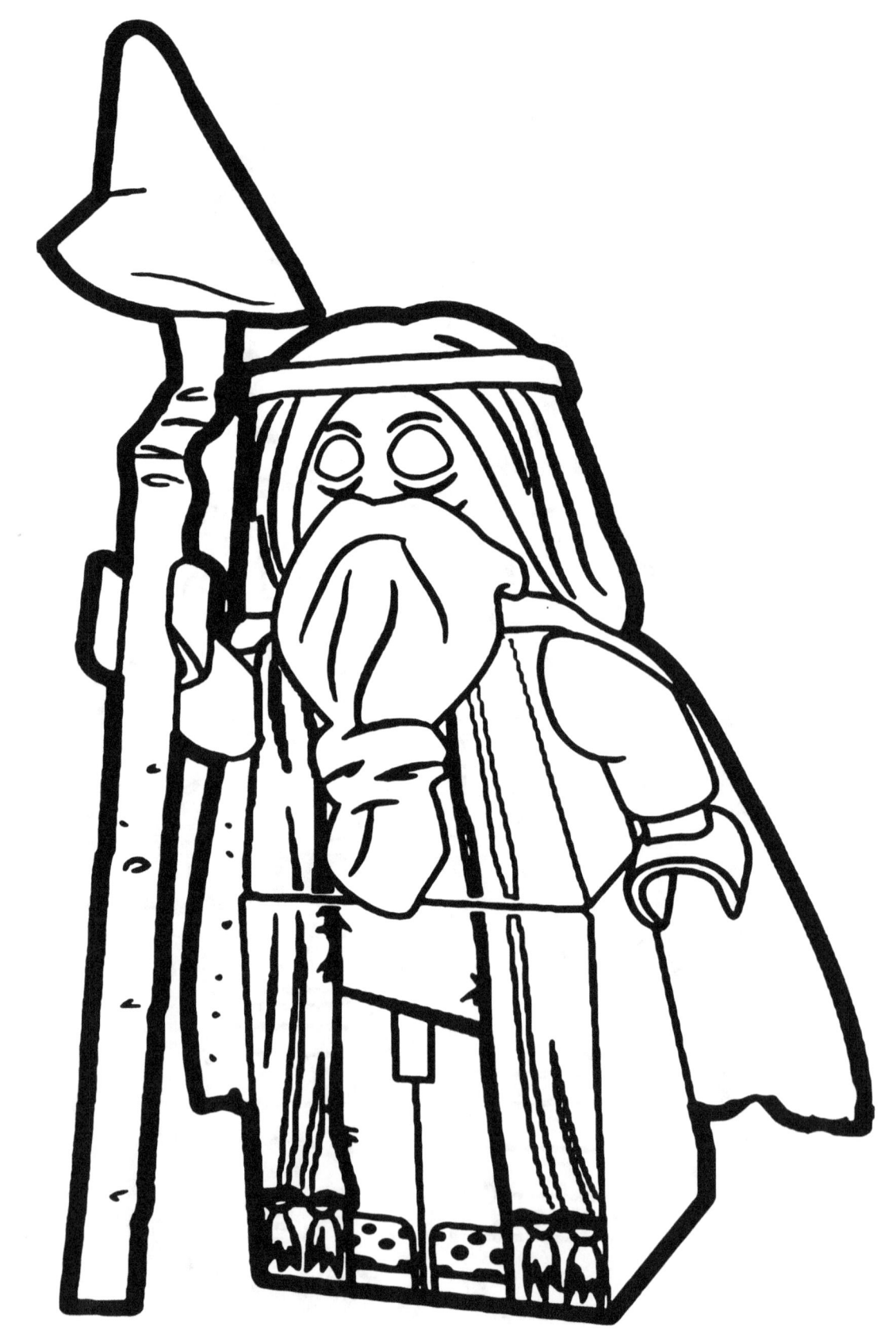

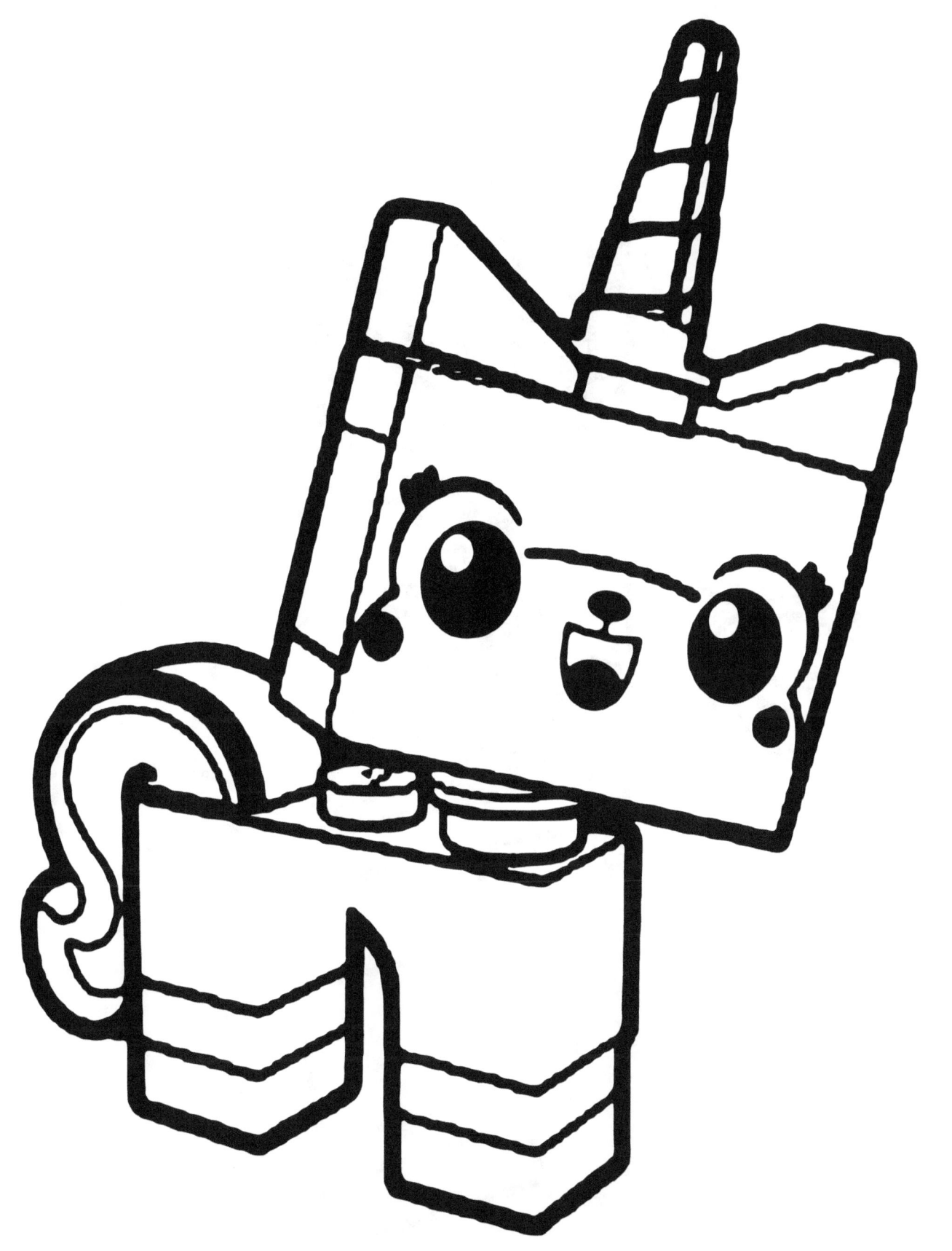

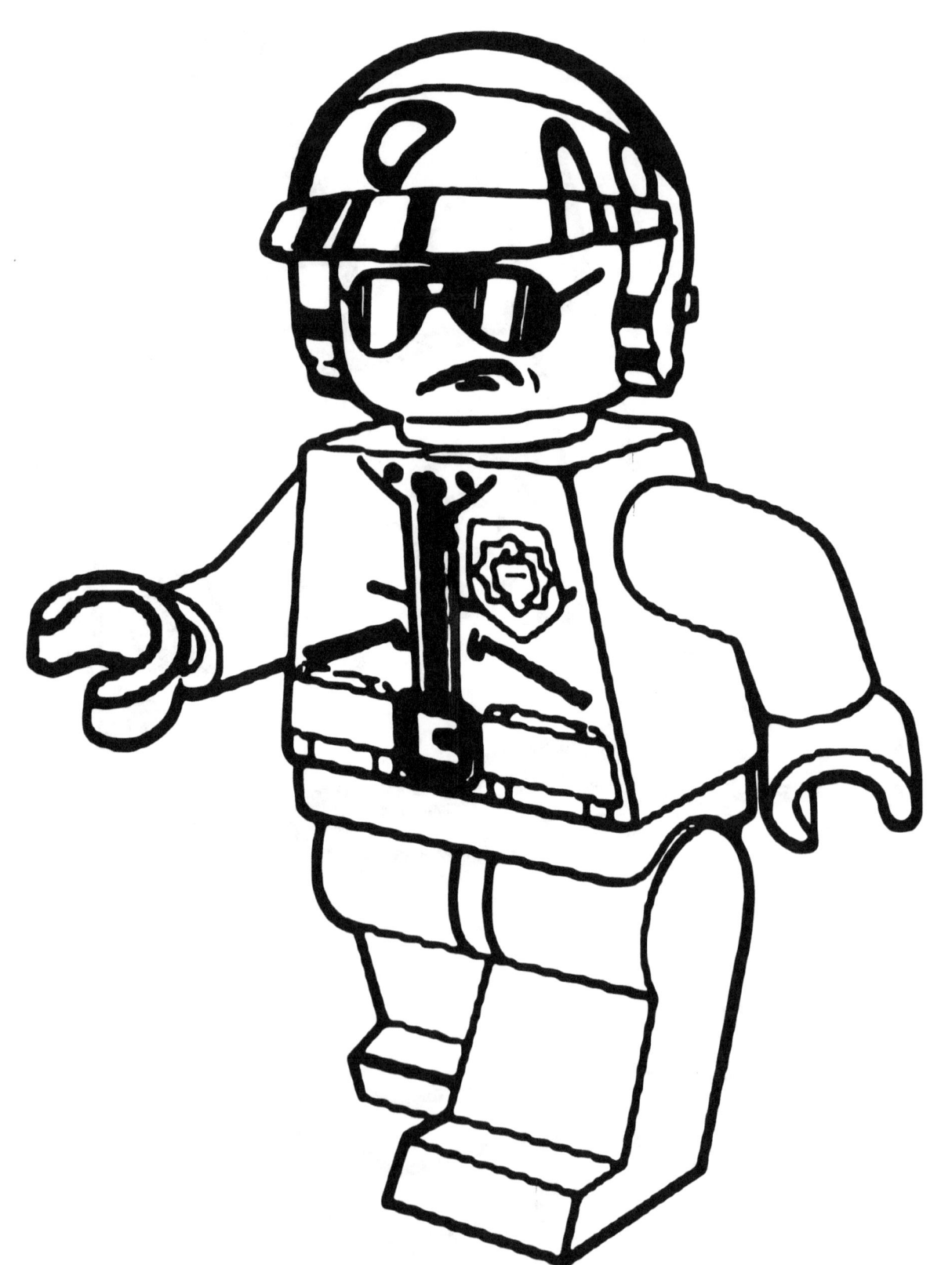

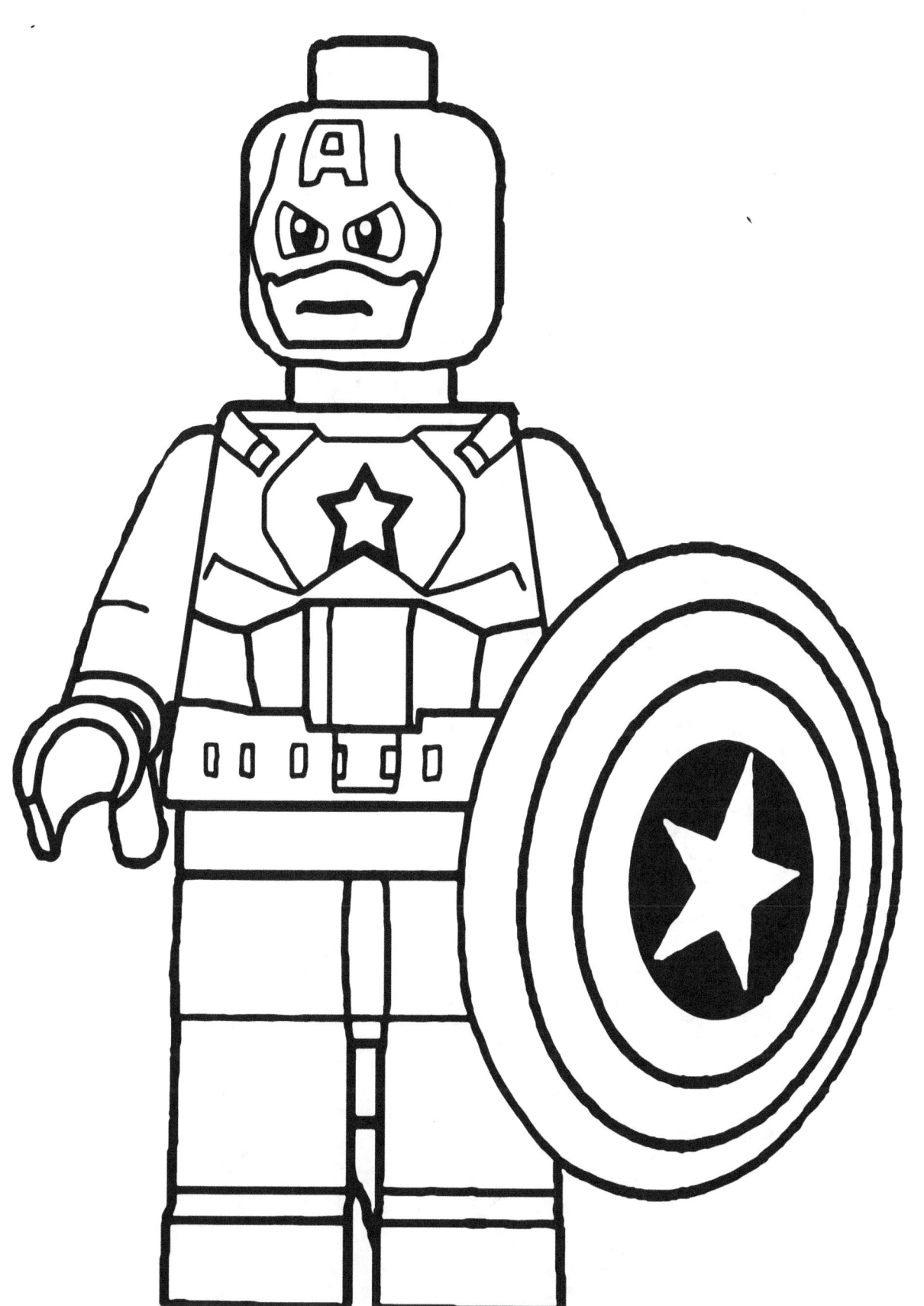

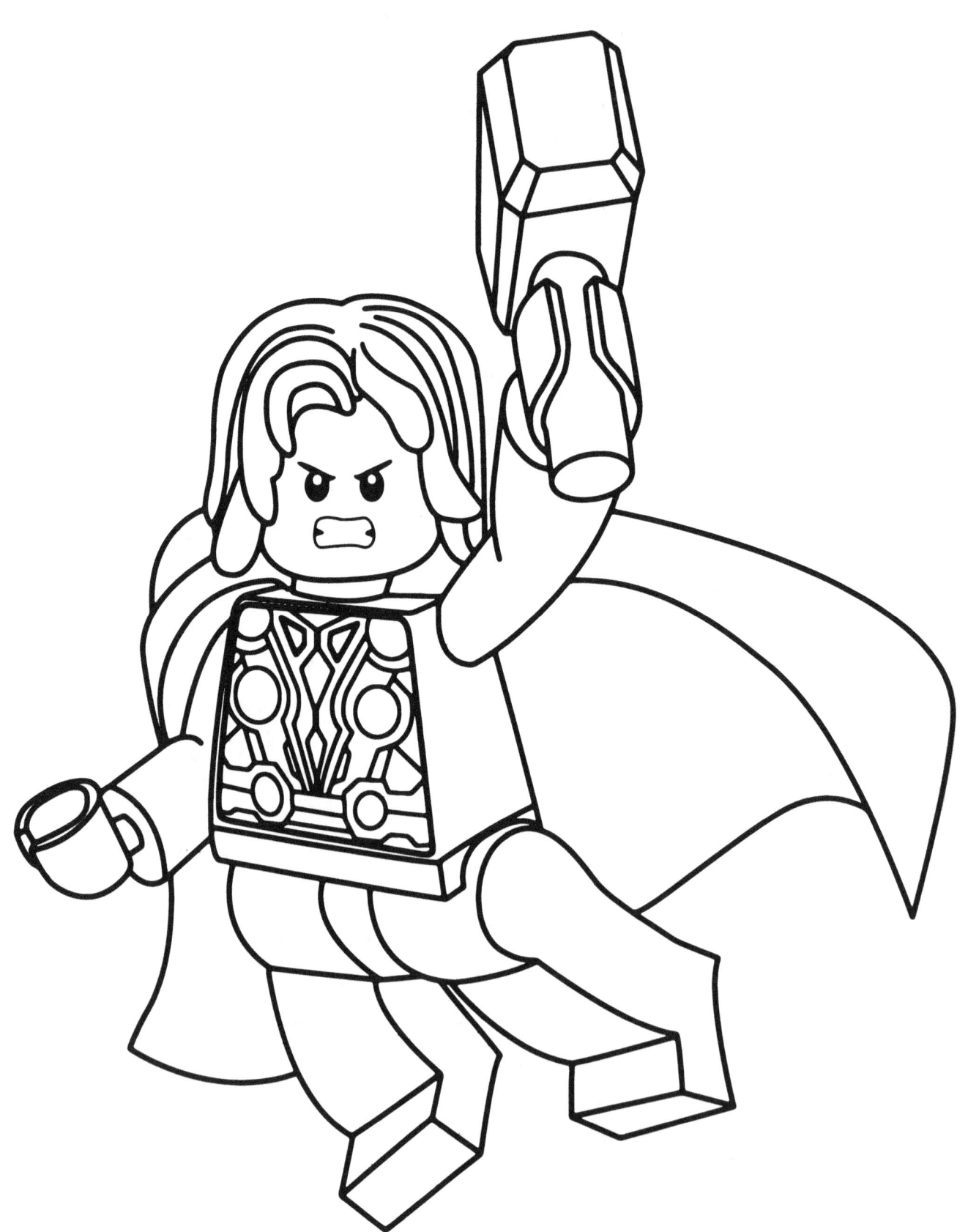

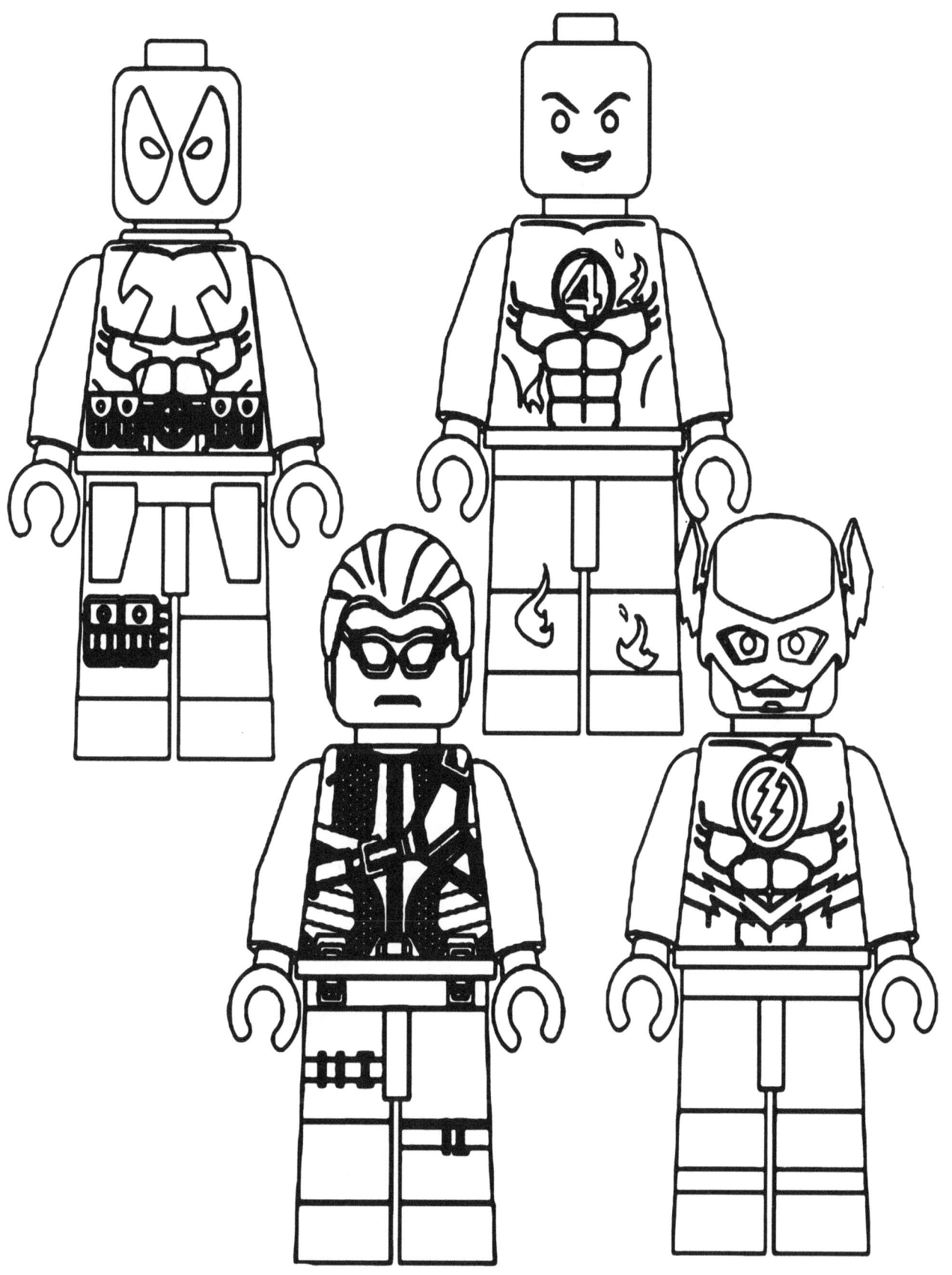

ISBN-13:978-1535202626
ISBN-10:1535202629